NO RETREAT SURRENDER!

Words Ignite Destiny: Speak Power, Speak Truth, and
Watch the Impossible Unfold!

BY
ALLIANCE B. ASABA

Library of Congress Reg. # 2025919208

Cover Design by: Authors Hike

Publisher: Authors Hike

For permission requests, please contact: asabaalliance@gmail.com

Dedication

To the fighters, the believers, and those who never give up—your words shape your world.
To my family, whose love and support have been my rock, this is for you.

Acknowledgment

I am grateful to God for His guidance, mercy and grace every step of the way. A heartfelt thank you to my family and friends for your unwavering support. To my mentors, your wisdom and encouragement have shaped my journey in more ways than I can express. To my readers, may this book remind you of the power of your words and inspire you to use them wisely. Speak with purpose, believe in yourself, and never stop moving forward.

Table of Contents

Chapter 1
The Words That Shape Your Life

"Words are free. It's how you use them that may cost you."
– Kushandwizdom

The Invisible Architect of Your Life

The first time I truly understood the power of words was when I was a child. It was a quiet evening, and my father sat at the kitchen table, flipping through an old, faded book.

The dim light cast a warm glow on his face as he looked up at me and said,

"Your words will build the world you live in. Choose them carefully; know that your words do not return void to you."

At that age, I didn't grasp the gravity of his words. I shrugged it off, thinking it was just another one of those parental sayings meant to keep kids from talking back. But as I grew older, I realized he was speaking a truth that would shape the course of my life.

I would later discover that words are more than sounds we make— they are the foundation upon which our identities, experiences, and futures are built.

The Night That Changed Everything

There was one particular night when those words came rushing back to me with full force. It was the night before my high school debate competition. I had spent weeks preparing, reading books, memorizing facts, and crafting arguments. But despite all the preparation, fear gnawed at my confidence.

I paced in my bedroom, whispering to myself,

"I'm going to mess up. I know it. My words are going to fail me. I can't do this."

My father overheard me from the doorway.

"Ma fille!"

He said, stepping inside,

"Whatever you voice, you attract; *if you keep telling yourself that, it will come true."*

I scoffed.

"That's not how it works. It's not like my words are magic."

He leaned against the doorframe and studied me for a moment.

"A man once told me, 'Life and death are in the power of the tongue.' It took me years to understand what he meant. The words you say to yourself, the things you believe about yourself, they shape you."

I wanted to dismiss his words, but deep down, something about them resonated. Could my own words be the reason I was feeling this fear? Could they be the very thing holding me back?

The Weight of Words

Words are not just sounds or letters strung together. They are the unseen architects of our reality. They can build up, destroy, encourage, discourage, create, or dismantle. Words can kill or give life; they're either poison or fruit - the choice is ours. And the most dangerous words are often the ones we don't even realize we're speaking—to ourselves, about ourselves.

Think about it: how many times have you told yourself, *"I'm not good enough,"*

or

"I'll never succeed?"

How often have you believed those words, allowing them to dictate your actions, choices, and future?

The words we hear as children shape our identities. A child who is constantly told they are smart, kind, and capable will carry those words like a shield against the world's hardships.

But a child who grows up hearing,

"You're not good enough."

or

"You'll never make it."

May spend a lifetime battling the ghosts of those words.

Sarah's Story: The Artist Who Stopped Believing

I remember a girl from my childhood named Sarah. She was bright and full of life, dreaming of becoming an artist.

But every time she showed her drawings to her father, he would shake his head and say,

"You'll never make a living off that. Stop wasting your time."

I watched as Sarah's sketches, once vibrant and expressive, became fewer and fewer. By the time we reached high school, she had stopped drawing altogether.

Was it because she lacked talent?

No.

It was because the words she had been fed had starved her of belief in herself...

The Science and Faith of Words

Science backs up what faith has been teaching for centuries—words hold power. Neuroscience shows that words physically alter our brain's structure. Positive words like *"I am capable"* or *"I am loved"* activate the brain's reward system, releasing chemicals that boost motivation and self-esteem. On the other hand, negative words trigger stress responses, leading to fear, anxiety, and self-doubt.

Faith echoes the same truth...

"Words can create or destroy lives!" – Proverb

Ancient texts and modern psychology both agree the words we speak determine the life we live.

How Words Shape Relationships

Our words don't just impact our self-perception; they shape our relationships. A simple compliment can brighten someone's day, while a careless insult can create wounds that take years to heal.

Think of the last time someone spoke encouragement into your life. How did it make you feel? Now, recall a time when someone's words cut deep. The emotions tied to those words linger far longer than we realize.

As author **Yehuda Berg** put it: *"Words are singularly the most powerful force available to humanity. We can choose to use this force constructively with words of encouragement or destructively using words of despair."*

The Unseen Impact of Negative Self-Talk

Many of us don't realize how often we engage in negative self-talk. These words become internalized beliefs that influence our decisions, self-worth, and success.

A study by psychologist **Dr. Shad Helmstetter** found that by the time a child is 18 years old, they have heard the word *"no"* or negative phrases approximately 148,000 times. Compare that to the number of times they hear *"yes"* or encouragement—it's not even close.

We must become conscious of the words we allow into our minds and the ones we speak about ourselves.

A Choice We Make Every Day

The good news is that we are not powerless. We get to choose the words we speak, the narratives we create, and the identities we claim. We get to rewrite the script that was handed to us, choosing words that build rather than break.

That night before my debate competition, I took my father's advice. Instead of repeating my fears, I stood in front of the mirror and said, *"I am prepared. I am capable. My words have power."*

It felt awkward at first, like I was trying to convince myself of something I didn't believe. But as I kept speaking, something shifted. The fear didn't disappear completely, but it loosened its grip. The next day, when I stood in front of my competitors, I spoke with confidence. I won that debate, but more importantly, I learned a lesson that would stay with me for life: The words we speak shape the world we live in.

A Challenge for You

Over the next few days, listen to the words you say to yourself and others. Catch the negative ones before they take root. Replace them with words of life, strength, and hope. Because the reality is words are not just expressions. They are seeds we plant in our minds, hearts, and the hearts of others. Whatever seeds we sow, we reap.

But this is just the beginning. Understanding that words shape our lives is the first step. The next step is realizing that every word we speak carries an unseen energy—one that either lifts us higher or drags us down.

In the next chapter, we'll explore The Power Behind *Every Word You Speak*. We'll uncover why words don't just influence our lives in the moment but leave a lasting impact that can shape generations. We'll examine real-life stories of people whose words created either monumental success or devastating failure. We'll also dive deeper into the connection between words and the subconscious mind, where lifelong beliefs are formed and where change truly begins.

So, as we turn the page, ask yourself...

What kind of energy are your words carrying?

And more importantly...

Are they moving you closer to the life you dream of—or further away from it?

Chapter 2
The Power Behind Every Word You Speak

"Life and death are in the power of the tongue." – **Proverb**

Words are more than just a way to communicate. They are the invisible forces that shape our lives, relationships, and destinies. Every word we speak carries energy, either positive or negative. We may not always realize it, but the things we say have the power to build dreams or tear them down, to heal or to harm, to encourage or to destroy. The impact of our words extends far beyond the moment they are spoken; they ripple through time, affecting not only our own lives but also the lives of those around us.

Imagine standing at the edge of a still lake, holding a small stone in your hand. When you drop that stone into the water, ripples begin to form, spreading out in every direction. This is exactly how words function. Whether they are spoken in anger, love, encouragement, or doubt, they continue to move through the world, influencing emotions, decisions, and even destinies. Words can either be weapons that cut deep wounds or tools that build bridges of hope and connection. The choice of how we use them lies entirely in our hands.

Reflect on the moments in your life when words have had a profound impact on you...

Perhaps someone once told you.

"I believe in you," at a time when you were struggling to believe in yourself.

Those words likely gave you the strength to push forward and prove your capabilities. Conversely, negative words may have sown seeds of doubt, making you question your worth. Words shape our identity, confidence, and aspirations. What we hear and say forms the foundation of our beliefs.

Research shows that words can change brain chemistry. Positive affirmations activate brain areas linked to motivation and resilience, while negative words trigger stress, fear, and anxiety. Therefore, what we say influences our subconscious, guiding our actions and shaping our future.

This chapter explores the importance of words, their interaction with our subconscious, and how careful word choice can transform lives. We will examine examples of individuals who used words to achieve greatness and those who were negatively affected by destructive speech.

By the end, you will understand the responsibility of your words and the potential to create a positive, purposeful, and successful life.

The Echo of Words: How They Shape Reality

Think about a time when someone said something to you that stuck with you for years. Maybe a teacher once told you that you were gifted, and those words pushed you to believe in yourself. Or perhaps someone spoke negatively to you, planting seeds of doubt that still haunt you today.

The words we hear, especially when we are young, leave an imprint on our hearts. They can push us toward greatness or keep us trapped in fear, influencing not just our thoughts but also our actions, decisions, and self-image.

Consider a child who repeatedly hears.

"You are smart and capable."

That child is likely to grow up with confidence, willing to take risks, and push through challenges…

Now, think of another child who constantly hears, *"You'll never amount to anything."*

Such words become ingrained in the subconscious mind, leading to self-doubt, insecurity, and a fear of failure. These echoes of words, whether positive or negative, create the foundation upon which we build our lives.

Scientific studies have shown that words can literally change the way our brains are wired. **Dr. Andrew Newberg**, a neuroscientist, conducted research that shows words profoundly shape brain activity. Positive words activate the brain's motivational center, releasing chemicals like dopamine that encourage action, persistence, and confidence. They enhance cognitive function, improve mood, and strengthen neural pathways associated with success.

Conversely, negative words trigger the brain's stress response, releasing cortisol, the hormone responsible for fear and anxiety. When exposed to repeated negativity, the brain's structure changes, reinforcing patterns of worry, self-doubt, and hesitation. This can lead to a cycle where individuals expect failure, avoid challenges, and struggle with low self-worth.

The power of words extends beyond scientific explanations; it is evident in everyday life…

Consider an athlete who constantly tells themselves, *"I am strong, I am focused, I will win."*

That mindset builds resilience and determination, leading to peak performance.

Conversely, an athlete who often claims, *"I'm not good enough, I always lose,"* may struggle not due to lack of talent, but rather because they have mentally conceded defeat.

This principle applies to relationships, careers, and personal growth...

A boss who consistently tells an employee, *"You're doing a great job,"* fosters motivation and loyalty.

A spouse who says, *"I appreciate you,"* strengthens emotional bonds.

In contrast, toxic words in relationships, such as constant criticism or belittlement, can leave lasting emotional wounds.

Every word we speak—whether to ourselves or others—holds an unseen power...

It either nurtures success or fuels failure. The choice is ours. By being mindful of the words we choose, we can take control of our lives and intentionally shape our reality with purpose.

The Subconscious Mind: Your Inner Recorder

The subconscious mind absorbs everything we say, whether we are aware of it or not. It does not filter out what is true or false; it simply takes in words and stores them as beliefs. This is why our self-talk is so important.

The words we repeat to ourselves become the scripts we follow in life, shaping our decisions, confidence, and success.

As the famous saying goes, *"Whether you think you can or you think you can't, you're right."* – **Henry Ford.**

Envision two individuals getting ready for an important job interview.

The first person wakes up feeling a little anxious but determined. They stand in front of the mirror, take a deep breath, and say, *"I am prepared. I am confident. I will do my best."*

Repeating these words, they start to believe them. Their posture straightens, their heart rate steadies, and their mind focuses on success rather than fear.

Meanwhile, the second person wakes up feeling nervous. They sigh and mumble to themselves, *"I always mess up interviews. I'll probably fail."*

As they repeat these words, their shoulders slump, their breathing becomes shallow, and their mind fixates on past failures. By the time they arrive at the interview, they are already defeated in their own mind.

Both of these people are speaking their reality into existence. Their subconscious minds take those words as truth and influence their behavior accordingly. Those who expect failure will feel anxious, second-guess their answers, and possibly sabotage their own success. The individual who speaks with confidence will enter the interview with self-assurance, thereby increasing their chances of performing well.

This is not about magic or superstition...

It is about the power of belief and the way words shape our subconscious programming. Neuroscience supports this idea. Studies show that when we repeat positive affirmations, the brain releases dopamine, the neurotransmitter associated with feelings of pleasure and well-being, which enhances motivation and focus. Conversely, negative self-talk activates the brain's fear centers, increasing stress hormones such as cortisol, which can impair memory, decision-making, and overall performance.

To illustrate this further, consider the story of **Lisa**, a young woman who dreamed of starting her own business.

For years, she told herself, *"I'm not smart enough to be an entrepreneur. I don't have what it takes."*

Each time she thought about pursuing her dream, her subconscious mind reminded her of these words, reinforcing fear and hesitation.

But one day, Lisa decided to change her inner dialogue. She began saying, *"I am capable. I am learning every day. I will succeed."*

At first, the words felt unnatural, but over time, they transformed her mindset. She acted, enrolled in business courses, and eventually launched a thriving company.

The lesson is clear: *Our words program our minds to expect certain outcomes, and we naturally act in ways that confirm those beliefs.*

If we fill our subconscious with doubt and fear, we limit ourselves. But if we speak words of confidence and possibility, we open the door to success.

As the great philosopher Lao Tzu once said, *"Watch your thoughts, they will become words. Watch your words, they will become actions."*

Real-Life Examples of Words Creating Success or Failure

Many successful people attribute their achievements to the words they spoke over their lives. The power of speech extends beyond simple motivation—it shapes reality. The way we talk about ourselves and our future either propels us toward greatness or anchors us in limitation. The most successful individuals have used their words to declare their destiny long before they achieved it.

The self-fulfilling prophecy of success…

One of the greatest examples of the power of words is **Muhammad Ali**, the legendary boxer. He was famous for saying, *"I am the greatest."*

He declared it long before he ever won a championship. To the outside world, it may have seemed like arrogance, but in reality, it was a deeply rooted belief in his potential. Ali understood the connection between words, belief, and action.

By consistently affirming his greatness, he conditioned his mind to act accordingly. His training, mindset, and fights reflected that belief, and eventually, his words became a reality.

He once said, *"It's the repetition of affirmations that leads to belief. And once that belief becomes a deep conviction, things begin to happen."*

His unwavering self-talk transformed him into one of the most celebrated athletes in history.

Another powerful example is **Oprah Winfrey**, who grew up in poverty and faced numerous hardships, including childhood trauma and setbacks. But even as a child, she spoke of doing something great with her life.

She constantly declared, *"I am destined for something bigger."*

That belief, fueled by her words, carried her through adversity. Instead of allowing her circumstances to define her, she shaped her reality with intentional speech. Today, Oprah is one of the most influential and successful women in the world, proof that words can manifest into incredible achievements.

She once said, "Create the highest, grandest vision possible for your life, because you become what you believe."

She understood that envisioning her dreams would ultimately shape her future.

The destructive power of negative words…

"Just as positive words can build success, negative words can lead to failure." – **Proverb**

I once knew a man named **Tom** who constantly spoke of defeat over his life. He would say, *"Nothing ever works out for me."* It became his life's motto.

Whenever he faced difficulties, instead of looking for solutions, he reinforced his belief by saying, *"See? I knew this would happen."*

He had unknowingly trained his mind to expect failure, and failure followed him everywhere.

One day, a friend challenged him, saying, *"What if you're wrong? What if things could go right for you if you changed the way you talk about your life?"*

At first, Tom scoffed at the idea. But after months of hearing success stories from others who changed their words, he decided to try.

He started saying, *"Things are getting better for me."*

At first, it felt unnatural, but over time, he began to believe it. Small wins started happening, and eventually, his entire outlook changed. His words altered his mindset, and his altered mindset led to improved results.

The lesson is clear: *Words either build or break us. What we repeatedly declare about ourselves becomes our reality.* Choose words that construct a future filled with success and purpose.

The power of words…

<u>Do they hold meaning?</u>

<u>Have you ever noticed how the atmosphere shifts when someone brings negativity into a room?</u>

A single sentence like *"This will never work"* can drain the energy out of a conversation. You can almost feel the collective sigh, the loss of enthusiasm, the way shoulders slump ever so slightly.

But when someone confidently declares, *"We can do this!"* The energy shifts. Hope fills the room, people sit up straighter, and a renewed sense of motivation prevails.

That's because words carry energy...

They are more than mere sounds or symbols; they possess the power to inspire, uplift, or destroy!

They influence not only our inner world but also the people around us.

Author **Yehuda Berg** once said, *"Words are singularly the most powerful force available to humanity. We can choose to use this force constructively with words of encouragement or destructively with words of despair."*

This idea is not just philosophical—it has scientific backing.

Japanese scientist **Dr. Masaru Emoto** conducted groundbreaking experiments on water molecules to show how words affect energy. In his studies, he spoke positive words like *"love"* and *"gratitude"* to one set of water samples and negative words like *"hate"* and *"fear"* to another.

When he froze the water and examined it under a microscope, the results were astonishing. The water exposed to positive words formed beautiful, symmetrical crystals, reflecting harmony and balance. However, the water exposed to negative words became distorted, fragmented, and chaotic.

His work suggests that words have vibrational energy capable of influencing even the molecular structure of water. If words can do that to water, imagine what they do to us! Our bodies are made up of about *60% water*, meaning the words we speak and hear directly impact our well-being on a cellular level.

Positive words can promote healing, confidence, and vitality, while negative words can trigger stress, anxiety, and even physical illness.

Imagine two different scenarios: In the first, a teacher tells a struggling student, *"You are intelligent, and I believe in your potential."* Those words plant a seed of confidence, and over time, the student begins to believe in themselves.

In the second scenario, another teacher tells a struggling student, *"You'll never be good at this."* Those words become a burden, a mental block that limits growth. The energy of those words lingers, affecting motivation, self-worth, and even academic performance.

Dr. Wayne Dyer once said, *"What we think and speak about, we bring about."*

This truth applies in every area of life, whether in the workplace, at home, or in our personal growth; the energy of our words is constantly shaping our reality.

The question is: **Are we using words to empower ourselves and others, or are we unknowingly creating limitations?**

As we move forward, we must become more aware of the energy we bring into conversations. Our words can be fuel for growth and success, or they can be the very thing holding us back. The choice is ours.

Becoming Aware of Your Words

Now that we understand the power of words, how do we use them wisely?

The first step is awareness…

We must become conscious of the language we use daily because our words shape our beliefs, emotions, and, ultimately, our actions. Many of us don't even realize how often we engage in negative self-talk.

Consider this: Do you often say things like:

- *"I'll never get ahead."*

- *"I'm not smart enough."*

- *"I always mess things up."*

Or do you choose words that empower you, such as:

- *"I am learning and growing."*

- *"I am capable and strong."*

- *"I will find a way."*

It may seem like a small change, but it makes a huge difference. Words, whether spoken aloud or internally, influence how we perceive ourselves and the world.

Dr. Shad Helmstetter, a leading researcher in the field of self-talk, found that by the age of eighteen, the average person has heard **148,000 negative statements** about themselves but only **3,000 positive ones**. This imbalance significantly impacts self-esteem and personal growth.

The power of self-talk…

Let's imagine two people facing the same obstacle. **Sarah**, upon facing a financial setback, says, *"I'm terrible with money. I'll never be financially secure."*

Her words become a self-fulfilling prophecy—she avoids budgeting, ignores financial planning, and continues struggling. Meanwhile, **Michael**, who faces the same challenge, tells himself, *"This is a learning experience. I'm getting better at managing my finances."*

His words shift his mindset, encouraging him to seek solutions, educate himself, and improve his financial habits.

What we repeat, we reinforce!

If we repeatedly tell ourselves that we are unworthy, incapable, or stuck, our subconscious mind accepts it as truth. But if we intentionally shift our self-talk, we can rewire our brains to think differently.

As **Maya Angelou** once said, *"Words are things. You must be careful about the words you use and the words you allow to be used in your presence."*

Breaking the habit of negative speech…

Becoming aware of your words requires effort and self-reflection. Try this simple exercise: Carry a small notebook for a day and jot down any negative statements you say or think about yourself. You may be surprised at how often negativity creeps in.

The next step? *Rewrite those statements into empowering affirmations.*

For example:

Instead of *"I'm not good at this,"* say, *"I am improving every day."*

Instead of *"I always fail,"* say, *"Each setback teaches me something valuable."*

Instead of *"I'll never achieve my dreams,"* say, *"I am on my way to success."*

"Your words are powerful. When you change them, you change your

mindset, and when you change your mindset, you change your life."
– Proverb

As the great philosopher **Lao Tzu** wisely said, *"Watch your words, for they will become your destiny."*

A Simple Challenge: The 7-Day Word Shift

Now that we understand the incredible power of words, how can we begin to harness that power in our daily lives?

"Change starts with awareness, but transformation happens through action." – Proverb

To put this into practice, try a simple challenge for the next seven days. The goal is to shift your language, both internally and externally, to create a more positive and empowered mindset. Small changes can lead to life-altering results.

1. Start your day with a positive declaration.

The way you begin your morning sets the tone for your entire day. Instead of waking up and immediately focusing on stress, worries, or past failures, start with an intentional positive statement. Stand in front of a mirror and say something uplifting about yourself.

For example:

- *"Today, I will make progress."*

- *"I am capable and strong."*

- *"I have everything I need to succeed."*

This practice may feel awkward at first, but over time, your brain will begin to accept these affirmations.

As **Louise Hay**, the pioneer of positive affirmations, once said, *"Every thought we think is creating our future."*

19

2. Catch and reframe negative words.

Throughout the day, listen to your words and thoughts. Are you unknowingly using language that limits you? If you catch yourself saying something negative, pause and reframe it into something constructive.

For example:

- Instead of *"I can't do this,"* say, *"I am learning and improving."*

- Instead of *"I always mess up,"* say, *"Every mistake is a lesson that makes me better."*

- Instead of *"I am terrible at this,"* say, *"With practice, I will get better."*

As **Tony Robbins** puts it, *"The words you attach to your experience become your experience."*

Rewriting your internal script will change the way you see yourself and the world.

3. Speak encouragement to someone else.

Your words don't just impact you—they impact everyone around you. Take a moment each day to uplift someone with a kind word or a gesture of encouragement. You never know who might need to hear something positive.

For example:

- Compliment a co-worker on their efforts.

- Send a text to a friend reminding them how strong they are.

- Encourage a family member who is facing challenges.

As **Maya Angelou** once said, *"People will forget what you said, people will forget what you did, but people will never forget how you made them feel."*

A few kind words can change someone's entire day.

4. Write down three positive things about yourself daily.

Each night, take a few minutes to write down three positive things about yourself. It could be a strength, an accomplishment, or even a small victory from your day.

This practice rewires your brain to focus on the good, rather than dwelling on flaws or failures. Gratitude and self-affirmation have been shown to increase happiness and reduce stress.

5. The result? A mindset shift.

By the end of seven days, you'll likely notice a shift in your mindset, confidence, and even your energy levels. Words are powerful, and when used correctly, they can transform your life.

As the saying goes, *"Change your words, change your world."*

Inspiring Words, Changing Lives

If there's one thing to take away from this chapter, it's this:

"Positivity Breeds Success! The way you talk about your future shapes the path ahead." – **Proverb**

Every word we speak is a seed planted in the soil of our minds. We must decide whether we are planting seeds of hope and success or seeds of doubt and failure. Our words hold the power to build or break, to inspire or discourage, to heal or harm. What we speak consistently, we manifest in reality.

Consider the stories of those who changed their lives simply by changing their words. Many of the world's greatest leaders, athletes, and visionaries understood that speaking life into their dreams was the first step toward making them real.

"Your words become your reality," said **Les Brown**, one of the most influential motivational speakers. This is not just an abstract idea—it is a principle backed by religion and centuries of human experience.

Reflect on the moments in your own life when words have shaped your confidence, relationships, or decisions. Maybe a mentor once told you, *"I see something special in you."* That phrase, even if it was spoken years ago, might still give you strength today. On the other hand, perhaps someone said, *"You'll never be good enough,"* and you've carried that weight longer than you realized.

But here's the good news: *You are not bound by the words of your past. You have the power to rewrite your narrative.*

The Journey Ahead

In the next chapter, we will dive deeper into the distinction between speaking life and speaking death—how the words we choose can either propel us toward greatness or hold us back in fear.

The choice is ours...

Will we speak words that create, or words that destroy?

The answer to that question will shape the rest of our lives...

Chapter 3
The Echo of Words – The Power We Hold

"The problems of the world could be solved overnight if men could get victory over their tongues." **– Billy Graham**

Words are more than mere sounds or symbols on a page; they are the architects of reality. Every syllable spoken has the potential to shape minds, change emotions, and carve the future. History is a testament to the power of words—some have built nations, while others have torn them down.

As the saying goes, *"Words are free. It's how you use them that may cost you."*

The true cost of words is often unseen: the relationships they mend or break, the confidence they build or shatter, and the hope they instill or extinguish. Words, whether whispered in love or shouted in anger, leave marks that time struggles to erase.

The ability to harness the power of words is one of the most profound skills any person can develop. Every civilization has been shaped by the spoken and written word. Religious texts, philosophical discourses, political speeches, and personal affirmations have dictated the course of history.

Aesop, the famous storyteller of ancient Greece, once said, *"No act of kindness, no matter how small, is ever wasted."*

This applies to words as well. A single phrase spoken at the right time can be the difference between despair and hope, failure and triumph.

The Irrefutable Power of Words Throughout History

Throughout history, words have been at the heart of change. **Martin Luther King Jr.'s** legendary *"I have a dream,"* speech did more than outline his personal vision; it wove a shared dream for humanity. Those words still breathe life into movements for justice decades later.

Winston Churchill, facing the terror of war, didn't rely on weapons alone—he armed his nation with words that emboldened them:

"We shall fight on the beaches... we shall never surrender."

Even in ancient times, orators such as Cicero and Socrates understood the profound impact of speech. Their words were not just used to persuade but to shape civilizations. A well-placed phrase has the ability to stir nations and mold the future.

"A single kind word can keep someone warm for three winters."
– Chinese Proverb

It reinforces the idea that spoken words hold power long after they are uttered.

Words have not only moved people to act but have also built and destroyed empires. The Declaration of Independence, the **Magna Carta**, and the **Gettysburg Address** are just a few examples of written or spoken words that changed the trajectory of history. These are not just collections of letters and syllables; they are catalysts of transformation.

The Story That Proves Words Can Change Lives

There was once a boy named **Ethan**, who grew up hearing the words, *"You are too weak, too slow, and too small to achieve anything great."*

The echoes of these words haunted him, embedding doubt deep into his soul.

One day, a mentor told him, *"Strength isn't in size, but in perseverance."*

That single phrase shifted his perspective. He carried those words into adulthood, becoming a record-breaking marathon runner.

This is not just Ethan's story. It is the story of countless individuals who have been shaped by the words of others. A well-timed encouragement can set someone on the path to greatness, just as a thoughtless insult can cripple potential before it ever unfolds.

A teacher who tells a struggling student, *"I believe in you,"* can inspire that student to achieve more than they expected. A coach who says, *"You have what it takes,"* can push an athlete to break records.

Napoleon Hill, the author of *Think and Grow Rich*, once said, *"Whatever the mind can conceive and believe, it can achieve."*

His words continue to inspire entrepreneurs, artists, and visionaries across the world. The words we hear, believe, and repeat to ourselves shape our futures in ways we often fail to recognize.

The Ripple Effect of Spoken Words

Once spoken, words travel farther than we ever anticipate. They create ripples in the fabric of reality, influencing people and events beyond our immediate reach. Consider the power of encouragement: a teacher's belief in a struggling student can transform their entire academic journey. Conversely, a harsh critique can extinguish the spark of ambition before it fully ignites.

Napoleon Bonaparte once declared:

"A leader is a dealer in hope."

Hope, often transmitted through words, has led revolutions and inspired generations. Leaders, parents, teachers, and friends all bear the responsibility of the words they speak, for they set the tone for futures yet to unfold.

A simple compliment or gesture of kindness can lead to an avalanche of positive changes. In contrast, a few harsh words spoken in anger can create lasting rifts. The ripple effect of words can be seen in daily interactions, whether through a kind message from a friend or a hurtful remark from a stranger.

The Science of Words and Their Impact on the Mind

Research indicates that words have a profound impact on our brains. Positive affirmations boost dopamine, enhancing motivation and resilience, while negative speech triggers stress responses, increasing anxiety and self-doubt.

Words have even been shown to affect physical health. Studies on plant growth suggest that plants exposed to encouraging words flourish more than those subjected to negativity. If words can affect plants, imagine their effect on human beings, whose emotions and identities are far more complex.

A recent psychological study revealed that individuals exposed to constant verbal criticism as children had higher rates of anxiety and depression later in life. Conversely, those who received consistent verbal encouragement showed increased confidence and success rates.

In a similar vein, the renowned psychologist **Albert Mehrabian** found that communication comprises only *7%* verbal content, while the remaining *93%* is conveyed through tone and body language. However, the impact of those words still holds the ability to dictate how people feel and respond in life. A slight shift in the way we communicate can change outcomes, relationships, and perspectives.

The Internal Dialogue That Shapes Your Destiny — *Self-Talk*

Perhaps the most powerful words are not those spoken to others, but those whispered to ourselves. *"I am not good enough." "I will fail." "I am not worthy."* These phrases, if repeated often enough, become self-fulfilling prophecies.

William Shakespeare once said:

"It is not in the stars to hold our destiny, but in ourselves."

The words we tell ourselves define the lives we lead. Science confirms that our self-talk influences brain function, confidence, and decision-making. Studies have shown that individuals who engage in positive self-talk experience lower stress levels, improved focus, and a greater likelihood of achieving their goals. Conversely, negative self-talk reinforces self-doubt and fosters a sense of failure.

Instead of **Muhammad Ali** (discussed in Chapter 2), let's consider the example of **Serena Williams**. She has always credited her mental strength and self-affirmations as a key to her success. From a young age, she trained herself to speak words of belief, repeating phrases like *"I am a champion"* and *"I will win"* before every match. Her words shaped her mindset, and her mindset, in turn, shaped her career, ultimately leading her to become one of the greatest athletes of all time.

Affirmations such as *"I am strong, I am capable, I will succeed"* rewire the brain, making success a self-fulfilling prophecy. The subconscious mind absorbs repeated thoughts, shaping reality according to what it hears most often.

We are constantly in conversation with ourselves. Each decision and action arises from this internal dialogue. The encouraging part is that we can modify the narrative. We can replace *"I can't"* with *"I will"* and transform *"I am not enough"* into *"I have everything I need within me."*

A **Buddhist Teaching** reminds us:

"The mind is everything. What you think, you become."

Our words—spoken, written, or thought—lay the foundation for the reality we experience.

The Eternal Legacy of Words

From **Nelson Mandela's** *"It always seems impossible until it's done,"* to **Mother Teresa's** *"Spread love everywhere you go,"* the world is shaped by words that outlive their speakers. Words are imprints on history, echoes that never truly fade.

A teacher's kind words may inspire a student to pursue greatness. A leader's speech can guide an entire generation. A simple compliment can brighten a stranger's day. Words are not fleeting—they are seeds, planted in the hearts and minds of those who hear them. Some seeds grow into forests of hope, others into fields of destruction. The choice is always ours.

Billy Graham's reminder remains a challenge to all:

"The problems of the world could be solved overnight if men could get victory over their tongues."

Imagine a world where words are chosen with care, where truth is spoken with love, and encouragement is given freely. The power to create such a world is in our hands—or rather, on our tongues.

The journey of life is not just about the steps we take, but the words we speak. With every word, we write the story of our lives. And as every great storyteller knows, the right words can change everything.

*With each word we choose, we set the course for what follows—**our future shaped by the echoes of our speech…***

Chapter 4
The Language of Faith and Possibility

"Faith is speaking the language of 'it is' when things look like it is not." – **Anonymous**

Throughout this book, we've journeyed deep into the realm of words, uncovering their profound ability to shape our realities, mold our self-belief, and leave an indelible mark on the lives of those around us. We've witnessed how words possess the power to tear down or construct, to discourage or ignite, to confine or liberate. Now, we arrive at a pivotal point in our exploration: the potent language of faith and possibility.

Faith, in its essence, transcends mere wishful thinking; it's an active, dynamic force. It involves speaking as if the desired outcome is already a tangible reality, claiming victory before the battle is won, perceiving the invisible, and embracing the seemingly impossible. When faith intertwines with the spoken word, its potency magnifies exponentially, capable of moving mountains, parting seas of adversity, and birthing long-held dreams into existence.

This chapter is dedicated to unraveling the intricate relationship between faith and words and how their synergy can pave the way for extraordinary breakthroughs. We will delve into historical accounts of spoken prayers and declarations that have altered the course of events, extract invaluable lessons from the lives of biblical figures and modern-day trailblazers, and equip ourselves with the tools to cultivate a daily practice of speaking possibility and purpose into our own lives.

The Potent Partnership of Faith and Words

Faith is not a passive concept; it's an active and dynamic force. It's more than just hoping for a favorable outcome; it's about **"expecting"** it with unwavering certainty, claiming it as your own, and speaking it into existence with conviction.

The Bible, in Hebrews 11:1, beautifully articulates this, stating, *"Now faith is confidence in what we hope for and assurance about what we do not see."*

Words serve as the essential vehicles that transport our faith from the intangible realm of the unseen into the tangible world of reality. They provide substance to our hopes and shape the very fabric of the experiences we encounter.

To illustrate this concept, envision the act of planting a seed. Faith represents the seed itself, brimming with the inherent potential for growth and eventual manifestation. Words embody the action of planting that seed in the fertile ground of the universe, providing it with the necessary foundation to take root.

As we nurture it with consistent belief, water it with unwavering expectation, and tend to it with a positive outlook, that seed begins to germinate, gradually sprouting and blossoming into the tangible reality we've spoken forth.

The Resonances of Faith in History

Throughout the annals of history, the language of faith has consistently played a pivotal role in shaping the trajectory of human destiny.

Within the sacred texts of the Bible, we encounter countless examples of individuals whose spoken faith triggered extraordinary and transformative results:

- *Abraham,* a central figure in biblical history, received a divine promise to become the father of many nations. Even before he had a single child, he was called Abraham, which means

"Father of multitudes." He continuously spoke this promise into existence, and against all odds, it came to pass.

- *Joshua and Caleb,* two of the twelve spies sent to explore the land of Canaan, demonstrated remarkable faith in their report. While the other ten spies focused on the obstacles and declared, *"We are not able to go up against this people, for they are too strong for us,"* Joshua and Caleb proclaimed, *"We are well able to overcome it."* Their words of faith paved the way for the Israelites' eventual victory and conquest of the Promised Land.

- *Jesus,* during his earthly ministry, frequently acknowledged the power of faith in the healing process. He would often say to those he healed, *"Your faith has made you well,"* recognizing that their belief in the possibility of restoration played a crucial role in their physical healing.

These timeless stories transcend their ancient context; they serve as powerful illustrations of a universal and enduring principle: words spoken in faith possess the remarkable ability to shape the course of reality.

The influence of faith-filled words isn't confined to the realm of religious texts; it permeates various aspects of human experience.

*"Consider the inspiring story of **Steve Harvey**…"*

When he was in the sixth grade, his teacher posed a seemingly simple question to the class: ***What do you aspire to be when you grow up?***

Steve, with a heart full of dreams, boldly declared that he wanted to be on television. However, his teacher, blinded by Steve's severe stutter, dismissed his dream as unrealistic and ridiculed him in front of the entire class.

Crushed but not Defeated, Steve shared the disheartening experience with his parents. His mother, a beacon of unwavering support and encouragement, countered the teacher's negativity with words of faith and affirmation. She instilled in Steve the belief that if he truly believed in his dream of being on TV, it would undoubtedly come to pass.

Today, Steve Harvey stands as a testament to the power of those faith-filled words, hosting 7 different TV shows and inspiring millions with his story of perseverance and triumph.

His mother's words ignited a spark of belief within him, a spark that fueled his arduous journey to success. He spoke his dream into existence, even when confronted with doubt, discouragement, and seemingly insurmountable obstacles.

The Mechanics of Manifestation: How Faith-Filled Words Work

To gain a deeper understanding of the mechanics behind how faith-filled words operate, we need to venture into the often-unseen realms of energy and vibration.

Everything in the universe, from the smallest atom to the largest galaxy, vibrates at a specific frequency. Our thoughts, emotions, and words are no exception; they all carry their own unique energetic signature. When we speak words infused with faith, we release positive, high-frequency vibrations into the surrounding atmosphere. These vibrations, in turn, interact with the Law of Attraction, a universal principle that posits that like attracts like.

In essence, when we consistently speak words of faith and possibility, we consciously align ourselves with the positive outcomes we desire to manifest in our lives. We emit a clear and powerful signal to the universe, and the universe responds by orchestrating a series of events, circumstances, and opportunities designed to bring our spoken words to fruition.

It's important to emphasize that this process isn't about engaging in magical thinking or wishful hoping. Rather, it's about cultivating a deep, unwavering conviction that empowers us to take aligned action, persevere through challenges with resilience, and maintain a positive and expectant outlook even when faced with seemingly bleak circumstances.

Overcoming the Obstacles to Faith-Filled Speech

If the language of faith possesses such immense power, why don't we all utilize it consistently and effectively?

What are the common obstacles that often hinder us from speaking words of faith and possibility?

1. Doubt

Doubt stands as the antithesis of faith, a formidable adversary that can undermine our best intentions. It's the insidious inner voice that whispers seeds of negativity into our minds, casting shadows of uncertainty with phrases like, *"It won't happen for you," "You're simply not good enough,"* or *"It's far too late to pursue your dreams."* Doubt has the potential to paralyze our tongues, effectively preventing us from speaking forth words of faith and possibility that could otherwise shape a brighter future.

2. Negative Past Experiences

Our past experiences, particularly those marked by disappointment and failure, can create a filter of negativity through which we perceive and interpret future possibilities. We may develop a hesitancy to speak words of faith, fearing the potential for repeated letdowns and disillusionment. The scars of yesterday can cast long shadows over the potential of tomorrow, hindering our ability to embrace the language of faith.

3. The Influence of Others

The people we surround ourselves with can exert a significant influence on our mindset and our words. If those around us consistently discourage our dreams, dismiss our aspirations, or mock our expressions of faith, their negativity can stifle our own ability to speak with conviction and unwavering belief. The power of social influence can either uplift or undermine our commitment to faith-filled speech.

4. Lack of Awareness

Perhaps one of the most common obstacles is a simple lack of awareness. Many individuals remain unaware of the immense power their words wield, especially when combined with the force of faith. They may engage in casual and careless speech, failing to recognize the profound impact their language has on shaping their lives and their destinies. This unawareness can lead to missed opportunities and unrealized potential.

Refining a Daily Habit of Speaking Possibility

Despite these common obstacles, the encouraging truth is that we possess the capacity to overcome them. We can actively cultivate a daily habit of speaking possibility and purpose into our lives, transforming our words into powerful tools for positive change. Here are some practical steps to guide you on this journey:

1. Start Your Day with Affirmations of Faith

The way you choose to begin your morning sets the tone for the entire day that lies ahead. Instead of waking up and immediately allowing your mind to be consumed by stress, worries, or dwelling on past failures, make a conscious decision to start each day with intentional affirmations of faith. Stand tall in front of a mirror, look yourself in the eyes, and speak positive and empowering statements about your identity, your cherished dreams, and the bright future that awaits you.

Some powerful declarations to incorporate into your morning routine include: *"Today, I will make significant progress toward my goals," "I am capable, strong, and resilient in the face of challenges," "I am blessed with everything I need to achieve extraordinary success,"* and *"My dreams are not mere fantasies; they are destined to come to pass in my life."* While this practice may initially feel awkward or unnatural, consistent repetition will gradually train your brain to accept these affirmations as your new reality. As the renowned author and speaker Louise Hay wisely stated, *"Every thought we think is creating our future."*

2. Pray Boldly and Specifically

Prayer represents a powerful form of faith-filled speech, a direct line of communication with the divine. When you engage in prayer, cast aside any hesitations or limitations and dare to ask for big things that align with your heart's true desires. Be specific in articulating your needs, your dreams, and your aspirations. Cultivate an unwavering belief that your prayers are being heard with attentiveness and compassion, and nurture a steadfast expectation that they will be answered in accordance with divine timing and purpose.

3. Speak Life Over Your Circumstances

Instead of succumbing to the temptation of complaining about the challenges and problems you face, make a conscious choice to speak words of faith and victory over them. If you're grappling with financial difficulties, declare with unwavering conviction, *"I am actively becoming debt-free,"* or *"Abundance is flowing into my life from expected and unexpected sources."* If you're confronting a health issue, affirm with unwavering belief, "I am healed and whole," or *"My body is strong, vibrant, and healthy."* Remember, your words have the power to reshape your circumstances.

4. Surround Yourself with Faith-Filled People

The individuals you choose to surround yourself with have a profound impact on your mindset, your beliefs, and the very words you speak. Seek out and cultivate relationships with people who actively encourage your dreams, wholeheartedly believe in your boundless potential, and consistently speak a language of faith, hope, and possibility. Their positive influence will uplift your spirit and reinforce your commitment to faith-filled living.

5. Guard Your Words Throughout the Day

Exercise vigilance over both your internal dialogue and your spoken words throughout the entirety of each day. Make a conscious effort to refuse to engage in negative self-talk that undermines your confidence or to utter words of doubt and fear that limit your potential. Instead, consciously and intentionally choose words that resonate with your faith, align with your desired outcomes, and propel you toward the realization of your dreams.

6. Testify to the Goodness of Life

Develop a consistent practice of acknowledging and declaring the positive aspects and blessings that enrich your life. This can be expressed through heartfelt gratitude, sincere praise, or simply by speaking openly and enthusiastically about the positive experiences that shape your journey. Make statements like, *"I am deeply grateful for the unwavering love and support of my family,"* *"I am blessed with incredible opportunities that open doors to growth and fulfillment,"* and *"I am surrounded by a community of love, kindness, and encouragement."*

The Power of *"I AM"*

Among the most potent and transformative ways to harness the language of faith is through the conscious and intentional use of "I AM" statements. The words that follow the powerful declaration of "I AM" carry immense creative power, shaping your identity and ultimately creating your reality.

- *"I AM strong,"* affirming your inner resilience and fortitude.

- *"I AM healthy,"* declaring vibrant well-being and vitality.

- *"I AM successful,"* embracing your potential for achievement and prosperity.

- *"I AM confident,"* embodying self-assurance and unwavering belief in yourself.

These declarations serve as powerful affirmations of your true identity and your boundless potential. They effectively program your subconscious mind for success, aligning your thoughts, beliefs, and actions with the positive outcomes you wholeheartedly desire.

Conversely, it's equally crucial to exercise mindfulness over the *"I AM"* statements you speak, both aloud and within the confines of your own mind. Negative "I AM" statements, such as *"I AM broke,"* *"I AM unlucky,"* or *"I AM always sick,"* have the potential to create a self-fulfilling prophecy of negativity, attracting undesirable circumstances into your life.

Therefore, choose your *"I AM"* statements with utmost care and intention, recognizing that they are the fundamental building blocks upon which you construct your future.

When Words Wound: The Importance of Empathy

While this chapter primarily focuses on the constructive and empowering use of words in the context of faith, it's imperative to acknowledge the other side of the coin: the devastating and long-lasting impact that negative words can inflict, particularly when they target someone's core identity and sense of self-worth.

I have personal experience with this...

When I was young, I loved singing...

I felt a deep connection to music...

And...

I discovered that I have a big, powerful voice that could fill a room...

However, my joy was often met with harsh criticism...

<u>Every time I would sing, my cousins, instead of offering encouragement, would shout at me with hurtful words:</u> *"Stop singing! Your voice is ugly, you cannot sing, and you are messing up the song."*

These words, spoken repeatedly during my formative years, inflicted a deep wound that has taken years to heal...

Even now, as a grown-up woman, the echoes of those negative pronouncements linger...

And...

I do not sing in public...

Even though I still cherish the act of singing in private...

This deeply personal experience poignantly reminds us of the immense responsibility we bear when we choose our words.

We must cultivate empathy, striving to speak with kindness, compassion, and a profound awareness of the potential impact our language can have on the hearts and minds of others.

Words have the power to build up or tear down, heal or harm, and it is our ethical imperative to wield them with wisdom and care.

Faith in Action: Real-Life Examples

The language of faith isn't merely a theoretical concept; it's a practical and transformative tool that has been effectively utilized by countless individuals throughout history to achieve extraordinary feats and leave an enduring legacy.

- *Mary Kay Ash,* the founder of Mary Kay Cosmetics, built a successful business empire by empowering women. Mary Kay was known for her belief in the power of positive reinforcement and encouragement. She created a culture where women were constantly affirmed and praised, contributing to their success.

- *Oprah Winfrey,* a media mogul and philanthropist who rose from humble beginnings and overcame a challenging childhood, understood the transformative power of words. Even in her youth, she spoke words of destiny and purpose over her life, consistently declaring, *"I am destined for something bigger than this."* Her unwavering faith, expressed through her powerful words, enabled her to rise above her circumstances and create a life of extraordinary impact and influence.

- *Joyce Meyer,* a renowned Bible teacher and best-selling author, has dedicated her life to empowering others through the message of faith and positive self-talk. She often emphasizes the significance of *"I can"* statements, encouraging people to boldly declare their abilities, talents, and potential, recognizing that their words have the power to shape their reality and unlock their God-given gifts.

These are just a few compelling examples that illustrate how the language of faith has transformed individuals' lives and propelled them to achieve seemingly impossible dreams.

A Call to Faith-Filled Living

The language of faith should not be regarded as a mere magic formula or a quick fix for life's challenges. Rather, it is a powerful and transformative tool that, when consistently applied, can reshape our lives, redefine our destinies, and empower us to live with purpose and passion.

It requires consistent practice, unwavering belief, and a courageous willingness to speak words of possibility even when circumstances appear bleak or contrary to our desires.

As we journey forward, let us fully embrace the language of faith in our daily lives. May our words be filled with unwavering hope, a strong sense of purpose, and the unshakeable conviction that our dreams are not distant fantasies but attainable realities waiting to be realized.

Remember this Truth: *What you consistently express, you attract into your life. Speak life into every situation and possibility into every challenge, and you will witness the extraordinary unfold and the impossible manifest.*

As we explore the power of words to uplift, a shadow lingers...

Words can create beauty and strength but also wounds, leaving invisible scars that cut just as deep...

What happens when the very tool meant for building becomes a weapon of destruction?

How do we mend the wounds inflicted by careless or malicious speech?

The solutions to these essential questions await!

Get ready to enter the sensitive and frequently painful area of verbal injuries as we pursue understanding, healing, and the resilience to overcome the pain.

The path to mastering the power of our words...

Demands that we confront not only their potential for good but also their capacity for immense harm...

Chapter 5
When Words Hurt – Healing from Verbal Wounds

"The tongue has no bones, but is strong enough to break a heart. So be careful with your words." **– Buddha**

The Echo of Pain: The Hurtful Power of Words

In the previous chapters, we've taken an extraordinary journey to explore the incredible power of words. Words shape our lives, carry energy, and can uplift and inspire us. Words are so much more than just sounds; they are the essential building blocks of our reality. However, we also recognize that this power can sometimes be turned against us; words can cause harm.

They can create wounds that, unlike physical injuries, often remain unseen yet linger on, profoundly affecting our lives. In this chapter, we'll explore the difficult truth about verbal wounds, looking closely at how words can hurt us, the different forms this hurt can take, and how we can start our healing journey. As we move from understanding the uplifting power of words to acknowledging their potential for harm, it's important to clear up a common misconception.

As children, we often hear the saying, *"Sticks and stones may break my bones, but words will never hurt me."*

This phrase encourages us to build resilience and learn to brush off insults. However, the reality is much more intricate. Words can truly hurt; they carry the ability to cause emotional and psychological pain that can often be just as, if not more, harmful than physical harm. In this chapter, we aim to unravel that misunderstanding and highlight the enduring effects of verbal abuse.

Recall a moment when words hurt deeply. It may not have been a heated argument; frequently, it's the nuanced remarks, the continuous belittling, or the silences that resonate most. These moments often leave lasting impressions on our minds.

I remember a time during college when I presented a project that I had truly poured my heart and soul into. The feedback from my professor wasn't outright negative, but it felt a bit dismissive. He used phrases like, *"That's an interesting approach,"* which, in his tone, seemed to convey the opposite. I can still recall that sense of deflation I felt. It wasn't just the words, but the underlying message that really chipped away at my confidence. That feeling of deflation and questioning my own capabilities lingered with me long after the class was over.

Why do certain moments and phrases stay with us long after they've passed or been spoken?

Words are so much more than sounds! As we've explored, they hold immense energy, sparking emotions, creating connections, and shaping our deepest beliefs. They have the incredible ability to uplift or bring down. When we encounter negative words directed at us, it can feel overwhelming, like a wave crashing against our inner calm. This can shake our sense of self-worth and cloud the way we see ourselves and the world. The effects may not be felt right away, but they can quietly creep in, subtly influencing our thoughts and feelings over time.

"Words are like bullets. If they escape your mouth, it is hard to take them back." – **Proverb**

This quote captures the lasting nature of hurtful words. Once spoken, they can't be retrieved, and their impact can stay indefinitely. They become a part of our internal narrative, shaping our thoughts and influencing our actions, often unconsciously. We carry these words with us, and they shape our interactions and expectations.

The Different Aspects of Verbal Wounds

Verbal abuse isn't always obvious. It's not just about yelling and name-calling. It manifests in many forms, some subtle and insidious. Recognizing these different forms is crucial for understanding the depth of verbal wounds and how to address them. Here are some common ways words can be used to hurt:

- **Insults and Name-calling:** This is the most direct form of verbal abuse, using derogatory language to demean, belittle, or attack someone's character. This type of attack aims to strip away a person's dignity and worth, leaving them feeling humiliated and vulnerable.

    o **Example:** *"You're a complete idiot." "You're so ugly." "You're a total failure."*

- **Criticism (Destructive):** While constructive criticism is all about helping someone grow, destructive criticism takes a different approach by tearing them down. It zooms in on flaws, often accompanied by harsh and judgmental words, without providing any helpful solutions or pathways to improvement.

    o **Example:** *"You always screw everything up." "Why are you so useless?" "That's a stupid idea, as usual."*

- **Threats:** These involve using words to instill fear or intimidate. Threats can be explicit or implied, targeting physical, emotional, or professional well-being. They create a climate of fear and insecurity, causing the victim to feel constantly on edge.

    o **Example:** *"If you cross me, you'll regret it." "I'm going to ruin you." "You'll never succeed if you leave me."*

- **Manipulation:** This involves using words in ways that can influence or mislead others. Often, manipulators take advantage of feelings such as guilt, love, or fear to achieve their goals. They may bend words and situations to increase their sense of power and control over those they target.

  o **Example:** *"If you really cared about me, you would..." "You're just being paranoid." "I'm the only one who truly understands you."*

- **Gaslighting:** A particularly tricky form of manipulation occurs when the abuser twists the victim's reality, leading them to question their own perceptions and mental well-being. This type of verbal abuse is especially harmful, as it undermines the victim's core sense of reality.

  o **Example:** "That never happened. You're imagining things." "You're overreacting. You're too sensitive." "You're crazy."

- **Dismissing/Invalidating:** This means downplaying or dismissing someone's feelings or experiences, which can make them feel unimportant or overlooked. It conveys the idea that the person's emotions are not valid or deserving of attention.

  o **Example:** *"Oh, just get over it." "It's not a big deal." "Your feelings don't make sense."*

- **Silent Treatment:** Refusing to communicate punishes and controls. This passive act inflicts emotional pain, creating isolation and abandonment, leaving the victim confused and desperate for connection.

  o **Example:** *A parent ignores their child for days following a minor disagreement, causing significant emotional distress.*

It's important to understand that verbal abuse can happen in any type of relationship, whether it's romantic, familial, friendly, or professional. Everyone can suffer from the impact of damaging words; identifying these patterns is the initial step toward liberation from them.

The Deep Wounds: *The Lasting Effects of Painful Words*

Verbal abuse can have devastating, lasting effects. Unlike physical wounds, the scars of verbal abuse may persist for years, affecting self-esteem, relationships, and overall well-being. The damage goes beyond the immediate sting of hurtful words.

I remember a dear friend who found herself in a long-term relationship where her partner often belittled her achievements and chipped away at her confidence. He would say things like, *"Anyone could have done that,"* or *"You only got that because you were lucky."*

Over time, she internalized these hurtful messages, making her hesitant to pursue new opportunities and causing her to second-guess herself, which diminished her self-worth. Even after the relationship ended, those words affected her future relationships and career choices. She carried these negative thoughts like a heavy weight, constantly questioning her deservingness of success and happiness.

The damage caused by verbal abuse can manifest in various ways:

- **Emotional Scars:** Verbal abuse can lead to a range of emotional difficulties, including:

    o *Anxiety:* Constant worry, fear, and unease, often stemming from the insecurity created by the abuse.

    o *Depression:* Persistent sadness, hopelessness, and loss of interest in life, resulting from the erosion of self-worth.

    o *Low self-esteem:* A diminished sense of self-worth and

value, leading to feelings of inadequacy and shame.

o *Feelings of worthlessness:* A deep-seated belief that one is undeserving of love, respect, or happiness.

o *Insecurity and difficulty trusting others:* A pervasive sense of vulnerability and a fear of being hurt again, making it challenging to form healthy relationships.

- **Psychological Effects:** In severe cases, verbal abuse can contribute to psychological disorders:

o *Post-traumatic stress disorder (PTSD):* Flashbacks, nightmares, and severe anxiety related to the traumatic experiences of verbal abuse.

o *Flashbacks or nightmares:* Reliving the abusive incidents, causing significant distress and disrupting daily life.

o *Dissociation:* Feeling detached from one's body or emotions as a coping mechanism for the trauma.

o *Difficulty concentrating and memory problems:* Cognitive impairments resulting from the chronic stress caused by the abuse.

o *Impaired decision-making:* Difficulty making choices due to self-doubt and fear of making mistakes.

- **Relationship Challenges:** Verbal abuse can significantly impair a person's ability to form healthy relationships:

o *Difficulty setting boundaries:* Trouble establishing and maintaining healthy limits, leading to further abuse or exploitation.

o *Trouble communicating needs:* Difficulty expressing

one's needs and desires, resulting in unmet needs and resentment.

o *Mistrust of others:* A pervasive belief that others will hurt or betray them, making it challenging to form intimate connections.

o *Higher chances of attracting or enduring further abuse:* A pattern of seeking out or accepting unhealthy relationships due to a distorted sense of what is normal or acceptable.

- **Physical Symptoms:** The chronic stress caused by verbal abuse can even manifest in physical symptoms:

o *Headaches*

o *Stomach problems*

o *Sleep disturbances*

o *Chronic pain*

o *Weakened immune system*

Words hold immense power. They can inspire or inflict deep pain and destruction. The wounds they create may be invisible, yet their impact can be devastating and enduring.

Starting on the Path to Heal

If you've experienced verbal abuse, it's essential to know that healing is possible. It's a journey that requires time, courage, and self-compassion, but you can break free from the cycle of pain and reclaim your life. The process is not linear, and there will be setbacks, but with persistence and the right tools, recovery is within reach.

1. **Acknowledge Your Pain:** The first and most crucial step is to

acknowledge the validity of your pain. Don't minimize your feelings or tell yourself that you're overreacting. Allow yourself to feel the emotions that arise, whether it's sadness, anger, fear, or confusion. Suppressing your emotions will only prolong the healing process and can even lead to further emotional and physical problems.

2. **Don't Blame Yourself:** Victims of verbal abuse often internalize the blame, believing that they somehow provoked the abuser. It's crucial to understand that abuse is *never* the victim's fault. You are not responsible for someone else's hurtful words or actions. The abuser's behavior is a reflection of their own issues, not your worth. Remind yourself that you deserve to be treated with kindness and respect.

3. **Seek Support:** Reaching out for support is a vital part of the healing process. Talk to trusted friends, family members, or a therapist. Sharing your experiences can be incredibly cathartic and validating. A therapist can provide professional guidance, coping strategies, and tools to help you heal. They can also help you identify unhealthy patterns and develop healthier ways of relating to others.

4. **Establish Boundaries:** Setting clear boundaries is essential for protecting yourself from further harm and creating a safe space for healing. This might involve:

   ○ *Limiting contact with the abuser:* Reducing or eliminating contact with the person who has been verbally abusive to minimize further damage.

   ○ *Ending the relationship if necessary:* Recognizing that some relationships are inherently toxic and that ending them is the healthiest option.

○ *Setting clear rules for how you expect to be treated:* Communicating your boundaries clearly and firmly, letting others know what behavior you will and will not tolerate.

○ *Asserting your right to say "no":* Recognizing that you have the right to decline requests or demands that violate your boundaries or make you uncomfortable.

○ *Communicating your boundaries clearly and firmly:* Expressing your boundaries directly and assertively, without apology or justification.

1. **Practice Self-Care:** Prioritizing your physical and emotional health is essential for healing. Participate in activities that provide joy, relaxation, and tranquility. This involves:

○ *Regular exercise:* Physical activity can help reduce stress, improve mood, and boost self-esteem.

○ *Spending time in nature:* Connecting with nature can have a calming and restorative effect on the mind and body.

○ *Pursuing hobbies and creative outlets:* Engaging in activities you enjoy can help you express your emotions and find a sense of purpose.

○ *Practicing mindfulness and meditation:* These practices can help you become more aware of your thoughts and feelings, allowing you to manage them more effectively.

○ *Getting enough sleep:* Adequate rest is essential for both physical and emotional recovery.

○ *Eating nutritious foods:* A healthy diet can provide your body with the nutrients it needs to cope with stress and heal.

2. **Challenge Negative Thoughts:** Verbal abuse often leads to

negative self-talk, where you internalize the abuser's words and begin to believe them. As we've discussed, our internal dialogue significantly impacts our self-perception. Actively challenge these negative thoughts and replace them with positive affirmations. Remind yourself of your worth, strengths, and capabilities.

3. **Forgiveness (Optional and Conditional):** Forgiveness is a complex and personal process. It's not always necessary or possible, and it should never be forced. If you choose to forgive, do it for yourself, not for the abuser. Forgiveness can help release anger and resentment, but it doesn't mean condoning the abuse or forgetting what happened. It's about freeing yourself from the burden of carrying that pain.

"To be wronged is nothing unless you continue to remember it."
– Confucius

This quote speaks to the burden of holding onto resentment and anger. Forgiveness, when it's genuine and comes from a place of healing, can free you from that burden and allow you to move forward.

Protecting Yourself: *Strategies for the Future*

Alongside recovering from past wounds, it's essential to establish strategies for shielding yourself from future verbal assaults. By learning to identify the indicators of verbal abuse and implementing strong boundaries, you can foster healthier relationships and avert additional harm.

- **Recognize the Signs:** Become aware of the various forms of verbal abuse. The more you understand how it manifests, the better equipped you'll be to identify and address it. Pay close attention to how others' words make you feel. If you consistently think belittled, demeaned, or emotionally drained after interacting with someone, it may be a sign of verbal abuse.

- **Don't Engage:** When faced with a verbal attack, it's typically wiser not to engage or defend yourself. Abusers usually aim to elicit a reaction. Responding can intensify the conflict and grant the abuser additional power. Instead, focus on staying calm and composed, and if you can, distance yourself from the situation.

- **Use "I" Statements:** Share your feelings and needs confidently, while avoiding blame. This way, you can express your viewpoint openly and make it easier for the other person to listen without feeling attacked.

  o **Example:** *Instead of "You always criticize me, "say" I feel hurt when I hear critical comments."*

- **Set Limits:** It's important to clearly communicate the behaviors you find acceptable and those you don't. Make sure the person understands that if the abusive behavior continues, you will need to step away from the situation. Being firm yet consistent in upholding your boundaries is crucial.

- **Remove Yourself:** If the abuse continues, it's important to consider taking a step back. You absolutely deserve to safeguard your well-being and prioritize your happiness. This might involve ending a relationship, reducing contact with a family member, or finding a healthier work environment for yourself.

- **Seek Help:** If you find yourself facing ongoing verbal abuse, please remember that it's really important to reach out for professional help or support from someone you trust. A therapist or counselor can offer you valuable tools and strategies to help you cope with the abuse and work on creating a safety plan that feels right for you. The best way to avoid getting hurt is to expect the worst, as per the famous saying below:

"Hope for the best, expect the worst" – **Angela Carter**

This highlights the importance of preparation, setting boundaries, and protecting yourself from harm. It emphasizes being realistic about potential abuse and taking proactive steps to safeguard your well-being, without expecting the worst in every situation.

The Power of Our Words: *Choosing to Speak Healing*

As we've highlighted, our words have incredible power. This power even reaches into our own healing journeys. The phrases we tell ourselves after facing verbal abuse can either keep the pain alive or help us move toward recovery. Our internal conversations are vital in shaping how we see ourselves and how we can heal.

- **Words of Self-Compassion:** Treat yourself with the kindness you would offer a struggling friend.

  o **Example:** *"This is a challenging situation, but I am strong." "I deserve to be treated with respect." "I am doing the best I can."*

- **Words of Affirmation:** Counter negative messages by reminding yourself of your worth and the value you bring to the world.

  o **Example:** *"I am worthy of love and respect." "I am capable of healing and growth."*

- **Words of Hope:** Stay optimistic and trust in your power to recover and build a brighter future.

- **Example:** *"I am hopeful about the future." "I believe in my ability to overcome this." "I am creating a life filled with joy and peace."*

- **Words of Empowerment:** Remind yourself of your inner strength and resilience.

  - **Example:** *"I am strong and capable." "I have the power to choose my own path." "I am in control of my own healing."*

Speaking self-compassionate and hopeful words is a powerful means to reclaim your narrative and promote healing. It involves consciously breaking the cycle of negativity with a supportive, encouraging voice.

Healing That Spreads: *Touching Lives Beyond Our Own*

Healing from verbal wounds involves addressing our own pain and choosing to use our words to heal and uplift others. We can become a source of comfort, support, and encouragement for those who have also experienced the sting of hurtful words.

- **Offer a Listening Ear:** Sometimes, the most healing thing we can do for someone is to listen without judgment simply. Let's create a warm and welcoming space for them to share their experiences and feel understood in their feelings.

- **Speak Words of Validation:** Help them understand that their pain is valid and that they're not by themselves in this journey. Reassure them of their intrinsic worth, and gently remind them that they truly deserve to be treated with kindness and respect.

- **Offer Support and Encouragement:** Offer practical assistance and heartfelt emotional support. Gently encourage them to seek professional help if they feel it's necessary, and take a moment to remind them of their incredible strengths and capabilities.

- **Be a Role Model:** By speaking with kindness, respect, and empathy, you can show others just how possible it is to communicate in a way that lifts everyone up, rather than causing hurt. *In your own interactions, it's wonderful to demonstrate healthy communication patterns!*

When we extend healing to others, we not only support them on their journey but also nourish our own healing process. This beautifully reminds us that we're not alone in our experiences and that we can truly make a difference by creating a more compassionate and supportive world with our words.

Healing or Harm: *Now You Decide*

We've journeyed together through the profound impact of words, both the uplifting and the challenging. It's remarkable how they can shape our realities, influence our feelings, and touch our relationships. We've also taken a closer look at the painful truth of verbal wounds and the lasting effects they can carry. *Now, here we are at this crossroads, and the choice is in our hands!*

Will we continue to wield words as weapons, perpetuating a cycle of pain and suffering?

Or

Will we choose to embrace the power of healing words, creating a world where compassion, empathy, and respect prevail?

The answer, I believe, resides in our eagerness to foster self-discipline in the way we communicate. It's about embracing the habit of taking a moment before we speak, thoughtfully reflecting on how our words affect others, and opting to express ourselves with wisdom and kindness. *Our words have the incredible ability not just to hurt but also to heal, restore, and uplift!*

As I reflect on the journey we've taken in this chapter, a chilling question hits my mind. It makes my heart pound and my palms sweat, forcing me to confront a terrifying possibility.

What if the words that hurt us most are those we say to ourselves?

What if the worst verbal abuse comes from our internal dialogue, the relentless self-criticism, self-doubt, and self-hatred we tolerate daily?

The implications of this question are staggering. If our own words have the power to wound us so deeply, then surely, they also hold the key to our healing and transformation.

How can we escape the cycle of self-inflicted suffering and learn to control the inner beast by fostering a voice of self-compassion and empowerment?

I suspect the answer lies in the ancient wisdom of controlling our tongue — a wisdom that will be revealed in the next chapter...

But until then, I am left with this unsettling question, hanging heavily in the air, a dark cloud on the horizon...

Let Your Voice Be a Force for Good:

"Your voice is one of your greatest tools.it is a vessel. A bridge between the soul and the world. It's free, its powerful, and it's uniquely yours. Every time you speak, you have a choice: to build or break, to encourage or discourage, to lead or follow. You call things into being. You don't need a stage to change lives. You just need intention. speak the truth with love. Speak blessings. Speak with faith, your words can heal, guide, and uplift. So from today forward, speak like your words matter — because they do. Be the person whose words people remember for the right reasons. Let your voice be a force for good, and watch what happens." As Rumi once said, "Raise your words, not your voice. It is rain that grows flowers, not thunder."

Chapter 6
Controlling Your Tongue – The Key to Peace

"You don't have to say everything you think. Sometimes silence is the smartest thing you can say." – **Mark Twain**

Let's take a moment to reflect. Often, we find ourselves speaking before really considering our words. We might let them slip out without fully being aware of the effect they can have. Whether it's due to stress, fatigue, frustration, or simply a common habit, it's easy for our words to race ahead of our feelings.

And here's a gentle reminder…

Once something is said, it can't be unsaid!

A small statement said in frustration can leave a deep wound…

A joke meant to be funny can hit someone's hidden insecurity…

A moment of thoughtless speech can create hours, days, or even years of regret…

This is why learning to control the tongue is one of the most powerful steps we can take if we want to live in peace, not just with others, but with ourselves.

Words are like little bundles of energy!

They have the amazing ability to shape our mood, influence our relationships, and even impact our future.

You have the power to choose your words wisely and promote peace!

As **Proverbs 15:1** says, *"A gentle answer turns away wrath, but a harsh word stirs up anger."*

That represents both the truth of the Bible and the truth of life itself.

One Moment That Taught Me Everything

One moment I remember clearly happened around the dinner table. I was tired, overwhelmed, and irritated by something small. Without thinking, I snapped at someone I care about. The room went silent. I watched their face fall. And immediately, I felt it—that drop in my stomach, that sting of regret. I didn't mean to hurt them. But I did.

And it hit me: *If I had just paused... If I had taken two seconds to breathe... it wouldn't have happened.*

That day, I started working on it...

Not to be perfect, but to be better...

Because...

Peace doesn't just come from what we do—it flows from what we say...

Why Controlling Your Words Matters?

If you don't learn to manage your tongue, here's what can happen:

- You say things you don't mean and damage relationships.

- You lose people's trust.

- You fill the air with stress, not peace.

- You fed drama that could've been avoided.

But when you choose to speak with wisdom, here's what happens instead:

- You create safety in your home and relationships.

- People listen when you talk.

- You become someone others can count on.

- You bring calm, even during conflict.

Proverbs 21:23 says, Those who guard their mouths and their tongues keep themselves from calamity."

<u>**That verse truly speaks for itself. Doesn't it?**</u>

The Power of the Pause

A pause is your best friend. It might not seem like much, but in that small moment before you speak, you take back control. You stop the spiral. You invite wisdom in. You choose peace over pressure.

Next time you feel frustration rising, try this:

1. Pause.

2. Breathe.

3. Ask yourself: "Is this helpful? Is this kind? Is this necessary?"

4. Speak with love, or stay silent.

*"Even our **Lord Jesus**, full of wisdom and grace, took a moment to pause. While others rushed in with loud voices and harsh judgments, He remained composed. He knelt down, drawing in the dust, choosing sacred silence over empty noise. And when He finally spoke, His words carried the kind of calm that quieted the storm and brought truth to the surface. His example reminds us that strength is not in volume, but in wisdom. "*

<u>**That moment of pause?**</u>

It's a skill to develop. Initially, it may feel uncomfortable. However, with consistency, it transforms into a habit and ultimately becomes a source of strength.

Say What You Mean, Without Being Mean

Controlling your tongue doesn't mean holding everything in. It means choosing words that convey truth and care. You can be honest and direct without being harsh.

It sounds like:

- **I feel frustrated**, but I want to talk this through.

- **I disagree**, but I'm open to hearing your side.

- **I need a break to cool off**, so I don't say something I regret.

Speaking this way builds connections, not walls. It lets the other person feel safe and respected, even when you're working through something hard.

When Words Become the Mirror of Your Heart

The words you choose have a powerful impact on how you feel. They can uplift your spirits and brighten your day, or, conversely, they can weigh you down. It's important to remember that the language you use matters, not just to others but also to yourself.

Embracing positive and kind words can create a more joyful mindset and foster a sense of well-being. You don't just use your words to talk to others. You use them on yourself, too.

And those quiet things you say in your head?

They matter more than you think...

If you're constantly telling yourself:

- I'm a mess.

- I can't do anything right.

- Nobody respects me.

That becomes your story!

But if you say:

- I'm still learning.

- I handled that better than last time.

- I'm doing my best, and that's enough.

Then your story changes, you change!

Instead of replaying the same doubts or whispering harsh words to ourselves, let's choose something higher. Let's build the habit of speaking life right into our own hearts.

Talk to yourself like someone who still matters...

Someone who's learning...

Someone who deserves patience and love...

The way you speak inside becomes the way you carry yourself on the outside. If your words are harsh, your world feels heavy. But if they're gentle, your whole spirit breathes easier.

Speak life for yourself and others, let your inner voice be the source of healing and peace...

Everyday Practice: Small Shifts That Matter

If you want to speak better, live lighter, and bring more peace into your days, try this:

- **Catch your triggers.** Are you snappy when you're hungry or anxious? Catch it early.

- **Breathe before you speak.** One deep breath can reset everything.

- **Affirm the good.** Instead of saying what's wrong, name what's working.

- **Apologize when you slip.** A quick, honest, sorry can fix a whole lot.

- **Speak kindly to yourself.** Always. Especially when no one else can hear it.

- **Practice stillness.** Sometimes, silence is the wisest word you can say.

The People Closest to You Feel It Most

It's a curious fact that we often communicate more sharply with those we care about the most. Perhaps it's because we feel a sense of safety in our relationships. Maybe we believe they'll always understand us. Or maybe we've become a bit too comfortable, forgetting that even the closest hearts can still be hurt by familiar voices.

Think about it: *Your spouse truly notices your tone more than anyone else. Your kids pay close attention to how you respond when you're feeling stressed. Your siblings carry the memories of things said during those heated moments. Your parents cherish your words long after a conversation wraps up. And your closest friends—they can sense your silence even more than your words!*

The people closest to us carry the weight of our words longer than we realize. What we say in a moment of tiredness or irritation might stay with them for days, even years. Strive to be the comforting haven they can lean on instead of becoming another burden in their lives.

Communicate as if their feelings truly matter because they absolutely do…

Allow your love to shine in its own unique way, as it truly deserves that…

A Lesson from My Grandmother

My **grandmother** often shared her gentle wisdom, reminding us that, *"You don't have to win the argument if you can win the peace."*

She was one of the softest talkers I ever knew, yet when she spoke, everyone listened. It wasn't about raising her voice; it was about enhancing the value of her words. She took her time to say, and was even slower to hurt anyone.

This taught me an invaluable lesson: *Wisdom whispers while foolishness shouts.*

What Peace Really Feels Like

When you take control of your tongue, something wonderful shifts deep within you. You start to feel a strength that doesn't need to shout. As you move through your day, you'll notice fewer regrets because your words become more thoughtful rather than reactionary.

The heavy weight of guilt that comes from speaking too quickly will begin to lift off your shoulders. You can finally let go of that burden of replaying conversations in your mind, wondering if you were *too harsh, too sharp, or too cold.*

Instead, you lie down at night feeling lighter. You remember how you handled that one moment calmly, how you chose peace over pride, and how you gave someone kindness instead of fire.

And here's the beautiful part—people start to notice. Not because you talk more but because your words carry more weight. Not because you try to impress but because your presence brings a quiet kind of wisdom.

You don't just talk differently. You live differently!

Five-Day Challenge to Reset Your Words

Build a new habit one day at a time. Change doesn't need to happen overnight; begin with one choice, word, or response. This challenge isn't about perfection—it's about being present and intentional.

Let these five days be stepping stones to a gentler, stronger you!

Day 1: Don't respond immediately to anything frustrating. Pause, breathe, and respond calmly.

Day 2: Encourage each person you interact with by saying something positive.

Day 3: Spend an entire day without complaining at all.

Day 4: Practice apologizing quickly if you mess up. Keep it short and sincere.

Day 5: Reflect on your feelings this week. What changed?

And remember, it doesn't stop here…

You can repeat this challenge as many times as you need. Every time you do this, you're reshaping your thoughts, nurturing your spirit, and creating a life that radiates peace, even amidst the chaos.

Take a moment to reflect…

At the end of each day, take a moment to note how you felt throughout the week. It's a wonderful way to reflect and connect with your emotions.

What shifted for you?

Did you feel calmer?

Did your relationships seem lighter?

Did you notice any changes in your perspective?

These little changes could be the first steps toward an incredible transformation…

Speak Light. Sow Peace. And Watch What Grows.

You don't have to rely on fancy words, deliver the perfect speech, or even have a big audience to make an impression.

<u>What truly matters?</u>

It's a heart that's eager to foster peace and a spirit that takes a moment to reflect before speaking.

Remember: *Your voice—yes, your very own—is one of the most powerful tools you will ever possess…*

With it, you can uplift spirits or create connections. You have the ability to either sow chaos or cultivate calm.

The choice is entirely yours!

Every word you speak is like a bit of seed, and each seed helps create the beautiful soil you'll walk in tomorrow.

So, speak with care and courage!

Embrace the kind of faith that believes in the importance of your words, because they truly do matter.

Let's plant peace…

Let's plant patience…

Let's plant love…

Allow your words to rise with grace and find their home in truth. Allow them to resound with the depth of your being, not as noise, but as wisdom; not from pride, but from a sense of purpose.

The next time you speak, remember that you're not just sharing words, you're actually shaping the world around you.

It's about creating a home, touching a heart, and building a future together...

That kind of power?

That kind of fire?

It lives on your tongue...

So, cherish it; nurture it with kindness, and use it to heal, bless, and uplift the atmosphere...

The mouth expresses what the heart truly feels. So, nurture a soft heart and choose your words with care. Remember, you are here to create *peace (one kind sentence at a time).*

Now, take a deep breath...

As we're just getting started...

The next steps will help you grow in ways you might not have expected.

Let's keep moving ahead together...

Chapter 7
Winning with Words – The Speech of Successful People

*"Good words are like deep water; smart sayings flow like a stream." – **Proverb***

Words are so much more than just sounds! They are the beautiful ways we express our thoughts, our feelings, and our desires. Words truly shape how we perceive things, guide our actions, and influence the world around us.

In this chapter, we're excited to explore the incredible power of words together!

We'll explore how some of the most successful people in history have used this power to do great things, inspire others, and really make a difference.

It's not just *what* you say, but *how* you say it, that makes successful people stand out. They've discovered the remarkable power of words to share their dreams, inspire excitement in others, and turn ideas into reality. When they speak, they do so with intention, clarity, and a refreshing sense of confidence that draws people in.

<u>Think about how words affect different areas:</u>

- ***World Leaders:*** The words of leaders can change countries, create friendships between nations, bring about change, and make peace.

- ***Business Owners:*** Smart business owners use words to describe their new ideas, create strong brands, and motivate their teams to work hard.

- *People Who Want Change:* The words of visionaries challenge the way things are, start movements, and help create a better future.

The Art of Talking to People

Some people possess a natural talent for language. They can capture an audience's attention, persuade even those who disagree with them, and leave a lasting impression.

A great example is **Nelson Mandela**. His words, whether in court during his trial or as president, showed his strong sense of dignity, his ability to bounce back from tough times, and his dedication to fairness. He used words to end apartheid, unite a country split apart by racism, and inspire a worldwide fight for equality.

Mandela's words had the power to:

- *Inspire Courage:* He made people brave enough to stand up to unfairness and fight for their freedom.

- *Create Peace:* He talked about forgiveness and getting along, bridging divides, and bringing people together.

- *Motivate Action:* He encouraged people to act, to stand up for what they believed in, and to work towards a more just world.

"To be free is not just to get rid of your chains, but to live in a way that respects and helps the freedom of others." – **Nelson Mandela**

Another good example is **Simon Sinek**. He's a well-known author and speaker who can explain complicated ideas in a simple but meaningful way. His words really connect with people, inspiring them to find their *"why,"* to lead with a purpose, and to build motivating organizations.

Sinek's words are known for:

- *Clarity of Purpose:* He stresses how important it is to have a clear reason for what you do.

- ***Focus on Connection***: He highlights how important it is for leaders to connect with people and understand them.

- ***Encouraging Action***: He motivates people to take action and become leaders themselves.

"People don't buy what you do; they buy why you do it. And what you do simply shows what you believe." **– Simon Sinek**

The Power of Believing in Yourself

Then there's **Serena Williams**, a powerful force in tennis and a symbol of self-belief. She has used her words to show complete confidence in her abilities, overcome problems, and inspire women and girls everywhere to pursue their dreams with passion and determination.

<u>Williams' words, often filled with confidence and the ability to recover from setbacks, show how language can:</u>

- ***Shape How You See Yourself***: She uses her words to define herself, creating an image of strength and capability.

- ***Influence How Others See You***: She earns respect and admiration, inspiring others to believe in her potential.

- ***Help You Achieve***: She uses words as a tool to reach her goals, both in her sport and in life.

"I really think a champion is defined not by their wins but by how they can recover when they fall." **– Serena Williams**

Words of Vision and New Ideas

Tyler Perry is a modern-day visionary who uses words not just to entertain, but to heal, empower, and uplift. Through his plays, films, television shows, and public speeches, he has become a powerful voice for hope, self-worth, and perseverance.

Perry speaks openly about struggle and success, about faith and forgiveness, and about the importance of dreaming big even when you start with little. His words reach across generations and backgrounds, offering encouragement to those who feel unseen or unheard.

Tyler Perry's words help to:

- **Describe His Vision**: He paints a vivid picture of a better world—one where everyone has a chance to rise above their circumstances. His stories often show people overcoming pain with faith and humor, building a future out of brokenness, and learning to believe in themselves again.

- **Inspire New Ideas**: Perry's message challenges people to look beyond what they see and imagine what could be. He pushes others to create their own paths, to think boldly, and to turn pain into purpose. Whether it's an aspiring artist, a single parent, or someone just trying to survive another day, his words plant seeds of hope and creativity.

- **Drive Progress**: Beyond words, Perry leads by example. He built one of the largest film studios in the U.S., on land that was once a Confederate Army base. He hires diverse casts and crews and gives opportunities to people often overlooked in the entertainment industry. His story shows how powerful words and consistent work can create real change.

Tyler Perry often reminds people that where you start doesn't define where you'll end up. He shares openly about being homeless, about rejection, and about the years it took to get his first play noticed. Through it all, his message never wavered: keep going, keep believing, and speak life over yourself and others.

"You can get a thousand no's, but all you need is one yes." – **Tyler Perry**

"I don't believe in luck. I believe in grace." – **Tyler Perry**

Perry's words continue to light the way for countless people chasing a dream, rebuilding after loss, or learning to love themselves again. In a world filled with noise, his voice stands out—not just for its strength, but for the love and purpose behind it.

Bring Your Future to Life

These people, and many others, understand that words don't just reflect what's happening; they are powerful tools that can shape it. They know that the language we use to describe our world, our situations, and ourselves has a big impact on what we believe and what we end up achieving.

The people we've talked about all had a clear vision, and they used the power of words to share that vision with the world. They spoke clearly, confidently, and with a passion that spread to others. They didn't just hope for success; they declared it into existence.

And this is a key lesson for all of us: What you say out loud holds the key to unlocking your greatest potential and making your dreams come true.

The Transformative Power of Affirmations

Many very successful people use daily affirmations and declarations to reinforce their goals, strengthen their beliefs, and develop a winning attitude. These positive statements, which you repeat regularly, help to program your mind for success and counteract negative self-talk.

Think of affirmations as seeds you plant in your mind!

If you take care of them by repeating them, these seeds will take root and grow, shaping your thoughts, your actions, and your life.

Here are some examples of powerful affirmations:

- *"I am in charge of my own life; I design my life with a purpose and plan."*

- *"I attract success, drawing opportunities that match my goals and dreams."*

- *"I have a source of inner strength and toughness that helps me overcome any challenge."*

- *"I am thankful for the abundance that comes into my life, both seen and unseen."*

- *"My potential is unlimited, and I am always growing and improving."*

- *"I radiate confidence and inspire others."*

- *"I am aligned with my purpose and passionate about my work."*

The Potent Force of Spoken Words

Affirmations work best when you speak them with real feeling and strong belief. It's not enough to say the words; you have to believe them and feel them deep in your heart.

Consistency is truly important!

The more you repeat your affirmations, the more they blend into your mind, and the more powerful they become. Try to make it a daily habit to share words of success, possibility, and strong belief over your life.

Remember, your words hold incredible power to shape your life. Choose them with care, speak them with intention, and see how your dreams soar and your goals turn into reality.

Speak It. Write It. Live It: The Blueprint of Success

Life is like a *grand symphony,* and your words are the instruments that create its melody. Just as a conductor leads an orchestra to produce beautiful music, you can use your words to create a life filled with *success, joy, and purpose.*

Imagine your words as notes on a musical score. Each word you speak contributes to the overall composition of your life. Positive, uplifting words create a vibrant and inspiring melody, while negative, self-defeating words generate a jarring and unpleasant tune.

Successful people are like master composers of their own lives. They carefully choose their words, understanding the profound impact those words have on their thoughts, feelings, and actions. They craft a compelling narrative of success, speaking their vision into existence with unwavering conviction and belief.

The Power of Proclamation

Proclamation isn't just about stating a fact; it's a lively expression of intent that adds color and passion to our communication. It involves sharing your dreams, goals, and aspirations as if they have already become your reality.

When you proclaim something, you're not merely expressing a wish; you're inviting the universe to join you in making it happen!

Consider the words of **Oprah Winfrey:** *"The biggest adventure you can ever take is to live the life of your dreams."*

Oprah didn't just dream of success; she proclaimed it. She spoke of her aspirations with such certainty and passion that they became a reality.

Oprah understood that our words have the power to:

- ***Define our Path:*** They set the direction for our lives.

- *Attract Opportunities:* They bring to us the people and situations that align with our vision.

- *Fuel our Determination:* They give us the courage and perseverance to overcome obstacles.

The Art of the Elevator Pitch

In the business world, the *"elevator pitch"* is a perfect example of the power of concise and compelling language. Entrepreneurs and innovators use this brief but impactful speech to describe their ideas, grab the attention of potential investors, and generate interest in their ventures.

A well-crafted elevator pitch, expressed with confidence and enthusiasm, can lead to funding, partnerships, and incredible opportunities.

It showcases the ability to:

- *Articulate Value:* Clearly and concisely communicate the value of an idea or product.

- *Persuade and Influence:* Capture the listener's attention and create a desire to learn more.

- *Inspire Action:* Motivate the listener to take the next step, whether it's scheduling a meeting or making an investment.

Words as Catalysts for Change

Words can be powerful catalysts for positive change in our lives and communities. They can inspire, uplift, and motivate us to act. When we share our thoughts and ideas, we create connections and spark conversations that can lead to meaningful transformation.

Let's embrace the magic of words together!

Throughout history, words have been a driving force for significant social and political change. Visionaries and activists have used the power of language to challenge *injustice, inspire movements, and transform societies.*

Mahatma Gandhi, the leader of the Indian independence movement, understood the power of nonviolent communication to bring about change. His words, filled with wisdom, compassion, and unwavering commitment to truth, inspired millions to resist oppression and fight for their freedom.

Gandhi's words taught the world that:

- *Words can be weapons:* They can be used to fight injustice and oppression.

- *Nonviolence is powerful:* Peaceful communication can be more effective than violence.

- *Change begins with the individual:* True transformation starts with changing our own thoughts and words.

> *"Be the change that you wish to see in the world."*
> **– Mahatma Gandhi**

The Ripple Effect of Positive Communication

Our words have a *ripple effect*, extending far beyond our immediate surroundings. They have the amazing ability to motivate and inspire everyone around us, creating a beautiful chain reaction that spreads outwards, warming the hearts of countless lives.

Mother Teresa, a *Nobel Peace Prize* winner, dedicated her life to serving the poorest of the poor. Her words, filled with compassion, love, and unwavering faith, inspired people around the world to embrace kindness, empathy, and selfless service.

Mother Teresa's words reminded us that:

- *Kindness is Contagious*: A single word of kindness can spark a chain reaction of goodwill.

- *Love Transcends Boundaries*: Words of love can bridge divides and unite people from all walks of life.

- *Service is Transformative*: Using our words to encourage service to others can change the world.

"Spread love everywhere you go. Let no one ever come to you without leaving happier." – **Mother Teresa**

The Symphony of Your Words

As you journey through life, remember that you are the conductor of your own symphony. Your words are beautiful instruments, and you possess the incredible power to create a remarkable masterpiece.

Choose your words with care, and let your voice reflect your intentions.

Share your vision boldly, with both courage and conviction!

Inspire, elevate, and craft a beautiful world filled with harmony and endless possibilities.

Let your voice shine bright!

In those peaceful moments when you take time to reflect on your life's journey, keep in mind that your words have beautifully woven the tapestry of your experiences. They've been the soft brushstrokes, adding vibrant color and depth to your relationships, shaping the contours of your achievements, and creating the soundtrack to your personal growth.

Your words can resonate through time, creating a beautiful legacy of hope, love, and inspiration. Cherish this incredible gift, and allow your voice to shine brightly, helping others find their own paths to success.

Let your words create a beautiful symphony of success, reflecting the tremendous power that resides within you...

Chapter 8
The Words We Speak to Ourselves

"You talk to yourself more than anyone else does—so make sure you're saying something worth hearing."
– Anonymous

Why Your Self-Talk Matters More Than You Think?

Many of us go about our daily lives with an ongoing conversation in our minds, often without even realizing it!

This isn't just a few casual thoughts here and there; it's a continuous narration of our experiences—a lively commentary on who we are, what we're up to, and our hopes for what lies ahead. From the moment our alarm clocks jolt us awake and we reach for our phones to those peaceful moments when we lie in bed, gazing at the ceiling as we drift off to sleep, that friendly inner voice is always there, ready to share its insights.

Sometimes, this inner voice acts like our own personal critic, quick to point out flaws and failures. It whispers doubts and fears, often sounding something like this:

- *"You're late again. What's wrong with you? Why can't you ever be on time?"*

- *"Everyone else is getting promoted, buying houses, starting families. You're falling behind. You're not achieving enough."*

- *"You messed up that presentation. You're not good enough for this job. Don't even try for that promotion, you'll just fail."*

These negative self-talk patterns can be incredibly damaging. They can chip away at our confidence and hold us back from reaching our full potential.

But the amazing thing is that the inner voice isn't always negative. It can also be a source of incredible strength and encouragement. It can be the gentle nudge that reminds us of our resilience, offering words of support like:

- *"You've faced tough challenges before, and you've overcome them. You're stronger than you think."*

- *"Take a deep breath. It's okay to feel stressed. Just focus on one step at a time. Keep going."*

- *"You are valuable and important. You matter, even when you make mistakes. Everyone messes up sometimes."*

The difference between these two internal voices isn't just about tone or the words used. It's much deeper than that. It's about the fundamental way we treat ourselves when no one else is around, when we think no one is listening. It's about the compassion and understanding—or the harsh judgment—we direct inward. This internal dialogue has a profound impact, shaping our career paths, the quality of our relationships, our physical and mental health, and even our spiritual beliefs. It influences how we perceive the world and our place in it.

Where That Voice Comes From

Here's a concept that might surprise you: that voice inside your head, the one that seems so uniquely "you," isn't entirely original. It's not something that is spontaneously generated within you at birth. Instead, it's a complex collection of echoes, a chorus of voices and messages that have accumulated over time.

Consider this: Your self-talk is shaped by:

- ***The words you heard growing up:*** The praise and criticism from your parents, teachers, coaches, and siblings. The messages you absorbed about your worth, your abilities, and your place in the world.

- *The experiences you've had:* The successes and failures, the moments of joy and heartbreak, the times you felt supported, and the times you felt alone. Each experience leaves an imprint on your inner voice.

- *The culture you've absorbed:* The subtle and not-so-subtle messages from TV shows, social media, movies, and the expectations of your peers. The cultural norms and values that shape your beliefs about what's "normal" or "acceptable."

- **The thoughts you've repeated:** The things you've told yourself over and over again, whether they're true or not. The more you repeat a thought, the more ingrained it becomes, until it feels like an undeniable truth.

As time goes by, all these different influences blend together to create the "automatic pilot" in your mind. This becomes the usual way you speak to yourself. Now, here's something really important: This automatic pilot doesn't wait for your okay. It just speaks up. It shares its thoughts and judgments without needing an invitation. And since it's always there, it has a strong effect on everything you do, think, and feel.

Let's consider some examples:

Imagine a **child** who constantly hears, *"You're too sensitive. Stop crying."* That child might grow up suppressing their emotions, believing that their feelings are invalid or a sign of weakness. They might develop an inner voice that tells them, *"Don't show your weakness, you'll be judged."*

Or picture **someone** who had a **coach** who repeatedly said, *"You're* *not built for this. You don't have what it takes."* That person might carry that message with them for years, their inner voice whispering, *"Why even try? You're just going to fail anyway,"* every time they contemplate pursuing a new goal.

Understanding the origins of your self-talk is the first step to changing it. You can begin to identify the sources of negativity and consciously choose to challenge those old, unhelpful messages.

Self-Talk and Mental Health: A Meaningful Connection

Self-talk is much more than a touchy-feely concept or a fluffy idea pushed by motivational speakers. *It's actually deeply connected to our mental health!*

The way we converse with ourselves can significantly influence our emotional well-being, stress levels, and overall quality of life.

Check out this undeniable link:

- *Negative self-talk fuels mental health challenges:* A critical inner voice fosters anxiety, depression, and chronic stress, keeping us alert and anticipating failure or rejection. This stress harms our mental and physical health.

- *Positive self-talk builds resilience and well-being:* Conversely, cultivating a kind, supportive inner dialogue equips us to navigate life's challenges. Positive self-talk fosters resilience, boosts confidence, enhances emotional regulation, and improves physical endurance. It helps us recover from setbacks, face rejection healthily, and experience less burnout.

Think of it this way:

Our brains are truly remarkable and incredibly adaptable! They learn and reinforce patterns over time. When you tell yourself daily phrases like *"I'm not smart enough"* or *"I always mess things up,"* you may unknowingly train your brain to expect disappointment. This can program your mind to look for and focus on any signs that support those negative beliefs, while disregarding any positive evidence that might contradict them.

Unfortunately, this can create a cycle where negative self-talk leads to negative outcomes, which only serves to strengthen that self-talk. *Let's break that cycle and embrace more uplifting thoughts instead!*

But here's an empowering truth: *You have the ability to break that cycle!* By consciously choosing your words, you can transform what your brain focuses on. You start to rewire your neural pathways, guiding your mind to notice your strengths, progress, and potential. This shift leads you from a mindset of limitation to one filled with possibility.

Let's Get Real: Everyday Examples of Self-Talk in Action

To truly grasp the power of self-talk, let's look at some relatable, real-life scenarios.

1. At School:

Jason is a bright and capable high school junior, but he freezes with fear every time he's called on to read aloud in class.

His inner voice, that relentless critic, bombards him with negative messages:

"You're going to stumble over your words. You'll mispronounce something. Everyone will laugh at you. You're just not cut out for public speaking. You're not smart enough."

This internal monologue devastates Jason's behavior. He avoids class participation, skips whenever possible, and feels intense dread and anxiety at the thought of engaging. His fear consumes him, hindering his focus and affecting his grades.

One day, his English teacher notices his distress and offers a simple but powerful note of encouragement:

"Jason, you have something important and valuable to say. Take your time. We want to hear from you."

That small act of kindness plants a seed of hope in Jason's mind. He goes home and decides to try something new. He begins to challenge his negative self-talk, replacing it with more positive and realistic statements:

"It's okay to be nervous. Public speaking is challenging for many people. I'm improving with each attempt. My voice and my ideas matter."

It's not a magical transformation. Jason still experiences anxiety, but his self-talk slowly shifts from fear to courage. He participates more in class, gains confidence, and discovers he has valuable insights to share.

2. In Parenting:

Maria is a single mom balancing a demanding job, a spirited toddler with epic tantrums, and unrelenting bills. She often feels overwhelmed and exhausted, as if barely keeping afloat.

During intense stress, her inner voice becomes a harsh taskmaster:

"I'm failing as a parent. I'm not enough for my child. I can't keep this up. I'm going to break down."

Negative thoughts fuel her guilt, anxiety, and despair, causing her to withdraw from friends and family, believing she's a burden and that no one understands her struggles.

One evening, amidst the chaos, her daughter suddenly wraps her arms around her and softly whispers, *"You're the best mommy ever. I love you so much."*

That heartfelt expression of love breaks through Maria's negativity, gently reminding her of her incredible strength and resilience.

Feeling inspired, she decides to start a nightly journaling routine, allowing herself the time to reflect on her day and wrap up each entry with a positive affirmation:

"Today was incredibly hard, but I showed up. I did my best. And that counts. I am a good mother."

Her life doesn't suddenly become easier, and the challenges still remain. However, by actively nurturing her inner voice, Maria cultivates a deeper sense of self-compassion and resilience. She accepts her challenges without allowing them to define her, thereby discovering a deep reserve of inner strength she had never recognized before.

3. In Health:

Ben has decided he wants to get back in shape. He joins a gym with enthusiasm, but almost immediately, the familiar loop of negative self-talk starts playing in his head:

"You're too out of shape. Everyone at this gym is in better condition than you are. They're probably staring and judging you. You'll never stick with it. You'll quit, just like you always do."

This internal barrage can make it tough for him to stay focused before he even gets started. He may feel self-conscious and discouraged, and sometimes, he might think about giving up. *But those feelings are completely normal!*

Rather than giving in to his negative self-talk, Ben takes a brave step.

He hires a personal trainer who offers guidance, support, and, crucially, positive encouragement. The trainer regularly reminds him:

"You're stronger than you think. You're making progress. You're capable of achieving your goals."

Ben begins actively changing his inner script, replacing negative messages with more positive and empowering ones:

"I'm showing up. I'm committing to my health. I'm building something. I'm proud of every small win, no matter how insignificant it seems."

He shifts his focus from perfection to consistency, joyfully celebrating his efforts and the progress he makes along the way, rather than fixating on any perceived shortcomings.

Months later, Ben not only feels healthier and stronger physically, but he also enjoys a profound transformation in his mindset. He thinks more healthily, filled with greater confidence and self-belief.

The Impact of Labels: Watch What You Call Yourself

Words have immense power, and this is especially true of the words we use to describe ourselves.

Every time you declare:

- *"I'm just lazy. I have no motivation."*

- *"I'm a complete mess. My life is always chaotic."*

- *"I'm not lovable. No one will ever truly care about me."*

- *"I'm too much. I'm too loud, too emotional, too sensitive."*

It feels like you're putting a label on your identity, which can really limit you and might not even capture the full picture of who you are.

85

Here's a really important truth to grasp:

You are not defined by your worst moment, your diagnosis, or your failures; you are a unique and multifaceted human being with remarkable strengths, some weaknesses, incredible potential, and intrinsic worth. Remember, you are so much more than any single label could ever capture.

Practice using observations that acknowledge your experiences instead of labels that confine you:

- Instead of *"I'm lazy,"* try *"I'm feeling unmotivated today."* This acknowledges your current state without making it a permanent characteristic.

- Instead of *"I'm a mess,"* try *"I made a mistake."* This recognizes that mistakes are a normal part of life and do not reflect one's inherent worth.

- Instead of *"I'm not lovable,"* try *"I feel hurt."* This acknowledges your emotional pain without making it a universal truth about your relationships.

- Instead of *"I'm too much,"* try *"I feel strongly about this."* This reframes your intensity as a strength rather than a flaw.

The simple act of separating what you feel or what you've done from who you are as a person is a powerful step towards healing and self-acceptance. It allows you to acknowledge your struggles without letting them consume your identity.

Language Shifts That Transform Self-Talk

Here are some practical language shifts you can make to cultivate a more positive and empowering inner dialogue:

Instead of Saying...	Try Saying...
"I'm terrible at this."	"I'm still learning how to do this. It takes practice."
"I always screw things up."	"Mistakes are how I improve. I can learn from this."
"I can't do this."	"This is challenging, but I'm willing to try."
"I hate how I look."	"I'm learning to care for myself with love and respect."
"Nobody cares about me."	"I'm worthy of connection and belonging."
"I'm not good enough."	"I am enough, just as I am."
"I'm a failure."	"I've experienced setbacks, but I'm not defined by them."
"I'll never succeed."	"I'm capable of achieving my goals with effort."
"I'm not strong enough."	"I have an inner strength that I can tap into."
"I don't deserve good things."	"I am worthy of happiness and success."
"I'm stuck."	"I have the power to create change in my life."
"I'm a burden."	"I bring value to the world."
"I'm not smart enough."	"I have unique talents and abilities."
"I'm unlovable."	"I am capable of giving and receiving love."

"I'm hopeless."	"I have hope for the future."
"I'm powerless."	"I have the power to make choices."
"I'm not worth it."	"I am worth it."
"I'm too old/young."	"My age is an asset."
"I'm not creative."	"I can express myself in unique ways."
"I'm not interesting."	"I have unique perspectives to share."

These small but consistent shifts in language can profoundly impact one's self-perception and overall outlook on life.

How to Practice Better Self-Talk Every Day

Changing your self-talk isn't something that happens overnight. It requires conscious effort, consistent practice, and a willingness to be patient with yourself.

Here are some effective strategies to incorporate into your daily routine:

1. Start Your Day with a Verbal Win:

Before you reach for your phone, before you get caught up in the day's to-do list, take a moment to say one positive thing about yourself out loud. It might feel a little awkward at first, but the impact can be significant.

Examples:

- *"I'm doing my best, and that's enough."*

- *"I bring value and positive energy to every situation."*

- *"I'm getting stronger, both mentally and emotionally, every day."*

- *"I'm capable of achieving great things."*

- *"I'm grateful for my unique qualities and talents."*

This simple practice sets a positive tone for the day and helps to counteract any negative self-talk that might arise.

2. Use a "Victory Folder":

Create a tangible collection of positive reminders. This can be a physical folder, a digital folder on your computer, or even a dedicated section in your journal.

Fill it with things that make you feel good about yourself:

- *Compliments you've received from friends, family, or colleagues.*

- *Thank-you notes or emails that express appreciation for your efforts.*

- *Photos of proud moments or achievements.*

- *Emails or messages that made you smile or feel valued.*

When your inner voice starts to turn harsh or critical, take a moment to review your Victory Folder. Let the evidence of your past successes and positive qualities help to silence your current doubts.

3. Talk to Yourself in the Second Person:

This might sound a little strange, but research has shown that it can be incredibly effective. Instead of saying, "I've got this," try saying, "You've got this. Keep showing up. You're doing great."

Why does this work? Talking to yourself in the second person creates a sense of psychological distance. It's almost like having a supportive coach or mentor encouraging you, rather than your own inner critic judging you. This creates psychological distance—almost like a supportive coach or mentor encouraging you rather than your own inner critic judging you. This subtle shift in perspective can make it easier to accept positive affirmations and believe in your capabilities.

4. End the Day With "3 I Did Goods":

Before you drift off to sleep, take a few moments to reflect on your day. Instead of focusing on what went wrong or what you didn't accomplish, ask yourself three simple questions:

- What is one thing I did well today, no matter how small it seems?

- What challenge did I face, and how did I respond?

- What decision am I proud of making today?

- This practice helps to rewire your brain to focus on your efforts, your resilience, and your positive actions rather than dwelling on errors or perceived failures. It cultivates a sense of accomplishment and self-appreciation.

5. Use the "Best Friend Test":

This is a simple but incredibly powerful tool.

Ask yourself:

"Would I ever say this to my best friend?"

Imagine your best friend came to you feeling discouraged, having made a mistake, or doubting their abilities.

Would you ever say to them:

- *"You're useless. You always mess things up."*

- *"You're so ugly. No wonder people don't like you."*

- *"You're so behind in life. You'll never amount to*

anything."

The answer is almost certainly a resounding *"No!"* You would offer them comfort, understanding, and encouragement. You would remind them of their strengths and their worth.

So, why would you accept such harsh and unkind words from your own inner voice?

Treat yourself with the same compassion and kindness you would offer to someone you deeply care about...

If you wouldn't say it to your best friend, don't allow your inner critic to say it to you...

What Happens When You Talk to Yourself Differently?

When you consciously and consistently choose to speak to yourself with kindness, understanding, and encouragement, the impact on your life can be transformative. You'll begin to notice some profound shifts:

- ***You Stop Waiting for External Validation:*** You no longer feel the constant need for other people's approval to feel good about yourself. Your sense of worth becomes more internal and stable.

- ***You Believe in Your Own Worth, Regardless of External Circumstances:*** Your self-esteem becomes less dependent on achievements or what others think of you. You recognize your inherent value as a human being.

- ***You Bounce Back Faster from Setbacks:*** When challenges and failures inevitably occur, you're less likely to get bogged down in self-criticism. Instead, you can offer yourself compassion, learn from the experience, and move forward with greater resilience.

- *You Dare to Dream Bigger and Bolder:* When your inner voice is supportive and encouraging, you feel more confident in your abilities and less afraid of taking risks. You allow yourself to pursue aspirations that you might have previously dismissed as impossible.

- *You Become More Willing to Try Again After Failure:* Setbacks are no longer seen as definitive proof of your inadequacy. Instead, they become opportunities for learning and growth, and you're more likely to persevere in the face of adversity.

Even Therapists Need This

It's important to remember that the struggle with negative self-talk is a universal human experience. Even mental health professionals who dedicate their lives to helping others cultivate positive self-perception have their own internal battles.

One *therapist* shared candidly, *"I spend my days teaching people to be kind and compassionate towards themselves, but there are definitely moments when the things I say in my own head are things I would never dream of saying to a stranger, let alone a client."*

This highlights a crucial point:

It's not about achieving some unattainable state of constant positivity or never experiencing negative thoughts. *That's not realistic.*

The key is to develop awareness—to notice those moments when your inner voice becomes harsh, critical, or unkind—and to consciously choose to respond with more truth, more kindness, and more intention.

Personal Reflection: What's the Story You're Telling?

Every single day, whether we realize it or not, we are narrating a story to ourselves. It plays quietly in the background of our lives like a steady rhythm, shaping how we see ourselves, what we expect from life, and how we move forward.

You are constantly telling yourself a story about:

- *Who you are – your value, your strengths, your weaknesses.*

- *What you can achieve – your goals, dreams, and potential.*

- *What your future looks like – your expectations, hopes, and fears.*

But here's the truth:

If the story you're telling is filled with fear, shame, doubt, or negativity, then it's time for a rewrite. You don't have to have it all together overnight. You don't need to fake joy or force yourself to become someone else.

The first and most important step is simply *awareness.* Pay attention to your inner dialogue. What are you saying about yourself when no one else is listening? What tone are you using? Are you speaking life or slowly tearing yourself down without even noticing?

When you become aware, you gain something powerful: *Choice.*

You can choose new words, shift the tone, speak from faith instead of fear, love instead of shame, and growth instead of defeat.

My father used to tell me:

"Be a woman who knows the power of your words. Be very careful of your tongue. Always use your words to heal, bless, and prosper."

That lesson stuck with me. Our words matter. They don't just describe our world—they shape it. They don't just tell the story; they *become* the story.

Sometimes, the wisdom we need is simple but deep:

"Examine what is said, not who is speaking."

"God has given us two ears, two eyes, and one tongue—so we should hear and see more than we speak."

And if you're wondering where to begin, listen to what's already coming out of your mouth.

*"Out of the abundance of the heart, the mouth speaks." – **Luke 6:45***

What's coming out will always reveal what's going on inside. That's not a reason for guilt—it's a guide for growth. If you hear anger, heal it. If you hear fear, face it. If you hear doubt, challenge it. If you hear power, hold onto it.

You get to choose the words that shape the story of your life. When you change the words, you begin to alter the outcome.

So, ask yourself:

What story am I telling today?

And is it leading me to the life I'm meant to live?

Your 7-Day Self-Talk Reset Challenge

Here's a simple week-long challenge to strengthen your self-talk:

Day	Focus	Practice
1	Awareness	Track 5 negative thoughts you say to yourself. Don't change—just notice.
2	Reframe	For each negative thought, write 1 empowering alternative.
3	Morning Declaration	Start your day with a positive "I am" statement.

Day	Focus	Practice
4	The Mirror Talk	Look yourself in the eyes and say 3 kind things aloud.
5	Speak Like a Coach	Encourage yourself out loud when things get tough.
6	Gratitude Shift	List 3 things you're proud of—not grateful for—*proud of.*
7	Record + Replay	Record a voice note to your future self. Listen back when you feel low.

Repeat this challenge regularly, embracing practices that resonate with you to grow into a compassionate, supportive inner companion.

Final Word: Talk Like Someone Who Believes in You

You don't have to fake it. You don't have to plaster on a superficial layer of positivity that doesn't feel genuine…

You simply have to tell yourself the full truth—the truth that you are worthy of kindness and understanding, that your effort matters, that trying again is a sign of strength, and that your voice, both inside and out, holds immense power.

Because in the end, you are the one person you live with most intimately, the constant companion throughout your entire life. Make that relationship a strong one, built on honesty, compassion, and unwavering encouragement.

Whatever story you keep telling yourself, day in and day out, you will inevitably start to believe it…

And in believing it, you will start to become it…

Now go forth and speak life to yourself…

Chapter 9
Words That Heal, Restore, and Rebuild

"Words are powerful containers. They can be filled with faith, hope, and love, or they can be filled with doubt, fear, and despair. What you put in is what you get out."
– Unknown

Alright, so we just spent the previous chapters till now wrestling with the toughest opponent you'll ever face: *The voice inside your own head.*

We pulled back the curtain on that non-stop inner conversation, the one that whispers doubts, shouts criticisms, and, if we're not careful, can be the source of the most brutal verbal abuse we endure. We saw how those internal words, the ones nobody else hears, shape your confidence, choices, and entire reality.

And I left you hanging with a question, didn't I?

It's a thought-provoking notion that resonates with many of us:

What if the words that wound us most are actually the ones we speak to ourselves? What if the true struggle isn't merely avoiding the harsh words from others but also quieting the persistent self-criticism, self-doubt, and self-judgment that we sometimes let roam free in our minds?

If our own words can wound us so deeply, leaving scars that no one else can see, then surely, they must hold the key to our healing, our freedom, and to putting ourselves back together, piece by piece.

That's precisely the direction we're taking now. We're emerging from the conflicts within our minds, yet we're carrying the strength of words with us. We're exploring the extraordinary, sometimes astonishing,

96

influence of words when we express them outwardly, using them to heal, restore, and rebuild—not only ourselves but also the relationships, communities, and dreams that seem shattered around us.

The same tongue that can destroy can also build...

The same voice that can hurt can also heal...

The Gentle Hand: Words That Heal

When considering healing, you might envision doctors, medicine, or perhaps time easing the pain.

<u>But what about words?</u>

<u>Can words genuinely heal something that is profoundly broken?</u>

Oh, my friend, you better believe it...

Think about a time you were flat on your back, perhaps literally sick or emotionally drained, feeling like you were drowning. Someone showed up – in person, on the phone, or via text – and said what you needed to hear at that moment.

Maybe it was a friend who said, *"Don't worry about a single thing. I'm handling it."*

Or maybe it was a family member who reminded you of a difficult time you overcame, highlighting a strength you'd forgotten. It was simply like, *"I'm thinking of you and praying for you."*

<u>Remember that spark?</u>

That lift in your spirit, knowing you weren't entirely alone in the dark...

That's healing...

Powered by words...

It's like that old saying, simple as dirt but true as the sky:

"A kind word is like a spring day." It simply melts the frost, thawing the frozen places in your heart.

This isn't merely a pleasant notion for a greeting card:

It's supported by science. Research indicates that Compassionate Communication—empathy conveyed through words and truly feeling heard—can reduce stress hormones such as ***Cortisol***.

Lower stress levels enable your body to concentrate on healing. When doctors employ empathetic language and clearly and kindly explain matters, patients frequently report reduced pain and often experience quicker recovery. Feeling acknowledged and validated leads to lower stress levels, positively affecting both physical and mental health.

Dr. Eli Mercer was a man of science, of tangible results and explainable phenomena. He'd spent decades navigating the labyrinth of human ailments, celebrated for his diagnostic brilliance. Yet, a subtle weariness had settled in his soul, a quiet disillusionment with the battles he couldn't always win, the suffering that medicine alone couldn't touch. His own internal dialogue had become a sterile echo of case files and prognoses.

One afternoon, he reviewed the case of a young boy, **Isaiah**, who was facing a particularly challenging illness. Isaiah's parents were understandably distraught, but Isaiah himself, whenever Dr. Mercer saw him, possessed a startling serenity. During one such visit, while Dr. Mercer was explaining a complex procedure to Isaiah's parents, Isaiah, who had been quietly drawing, looked up.

"Dr. Mercer," Isaiah said, his voice small but clear, *"my grandma says that even when the doctors are doing their best, the angels are also helping. And words are like little messengers for them."*

He held up his drawing – a colourful, somewhat lopsided depiction of a smiling sun with figures that looked like angels around a child in a bed.

Dr. Mercer, usually adept at managing conversations with patients and their families, found himself momentarily speechless. It wasn't a medical observation, nor a question about his treatment plan. It was a simple, profound statement of faith, delivered with the unshakeable conviction only a child can possess. *"Little messengers..."* He repeated softly to himself later that day, the phrase replaying in his mind.

Isaiah's innocent words, *"Words are like little messengers,"* began to chip away at the hardened shell around Dr. Mercer's professional heart.

He started to listen differently, not just to the clinical details, but to his patients' hopes, fears, and unspoken narratives. He found himself choosing his own words with more care, realising they weren't just conveying information but could indeed be *"messengers"* of comfort, hope, or shared humanity.

This shift didn't magically cure all his patients, but it began to heal something within Dr. Mercer himself – the part of him that had started to believe only in what he could see and measure. Isaiah's words reminded him of the unseen, the immeasurable power of connection and the spirit, and in doing so, they mended a part of his own weary soul, reigniting a gentler, more holistic approach to his practice.

Words are also crucial for spiritual healing. When faith is shaken by tragedy, loss, or the sheer weight of the world, words of scripture, prayer, or the simple and solid reassurance from a fellow traveler on the path can offer solace and reconnection.

The words *"You are loved," "You are not alone," "There is grace for this,"* and *"God is with you in this,"* can be profoundly healing to a wounded spirit, reminding you of a truth deeper than your current pain.

Putting Back the Pieces: Words That Restore

"Life happens, and sometimes, it happens hard on relationships."
– Proverb

Careless words, broken promises, and festering misunderstandings can leave relationships feeling bruised, cracked, or even shattered. Trust, built over many years—brick by painstaking brick—can feel like dust in the wind after just a few thoughtless comments or a moment of uncontrolled anger. The *silence* that settles in after a disagreement can feel louder and heavier than any *shouting*.

But here's the incredible thing:

The miracle we often overlook.

Words have a remarkable ability to break connections and mend them. While it can be challenging, requiring courage, humility, and the bravery to embrace vulnerability, the journey into that uncomfortable space is worth it. Despite the difficulties, the possibility of healing and rebuilding those bonds is truly significant.

The most powerful word for restoration?

Often, it's a simple, raw, *"I messed up."*

Followed closely by *"I'm sorry."*

And I'm not talking about the quick, mumbled *"my bad"* as you walk away. Not the defensive *"I'm sorry if you feel that way,"* which isn't an apology at all.

A real, gut-level, heartfelt apology takes ownership. It says, "I see that my words/actions hurt you. I own that. That was wrong. I am truly sorry for the pain I caused. I understand the impact. I value you and

100

what we have, and I want to make this right."

A genuine apology validates the other person's hurt. It says, *"Your feelings matter. Your pain is real."*

It creates a space for them to begin healing and lowering their defenses...

It's an invitation to rebuild and lay a new foundation...

Then there are the words of forgiveness. Offering forgiveness, whether to someone else or, just as importantly, to yourself, is a powerful act of release. It's a choice to cut the chain of anger and resentment that binds you. It doesn't mean forgetting what happened or saying it was okay. It means letting go of the bitterness that poisons your spirit.

Saying *"I forgive you"* can be the initial step toward rebuilding trust with someone or the final step to finding your own peace and moving forward, even if the relationship isn't fully restored.

Consider the story of **Evelyn** and her younger sister, **Rosa.** A chasm of bitter silence had stretched between them for nearly a decade, broader and deeper than any physical distance. It began with a misunderstanding over their late mother's cherished rose garden, symbolising their shared childhood.

Sharp, accusatory words had flown like poisoned darts, each finding its mark, leaving wounds that festered in the ensuing silence. Holidays passed with an empty chair, family news was relayed through awkward third parties, and the shared history that once bound them felt like a forgotten language.

Evelyn, the elder, carried the weight of her harsh words like a stone in her heart, while Rosa nursed the pain of feeling unjustly accused and dismissed. Both were too proud, too hurt, to make the first move. The silence became its monument to their broken bond.

Then, one spring, Rosa received a small, handwritten card from Evelyn. There was no grand excuse, no lengthy justification—just a few simple sentences: *"Rosa, the roses are blooming again, and they make me think of Mom and of you. I miss you. I was wrong to speak to you as I did. I am so sorry for the pain my words caused."*

Rosa read the card several times, her hands trembling. Evelyn's words, devoid of blame and filled with a raw vulnerability she hadn't seen in years, began to dismantle the brick by painful brick wall around Rosa's heart. It wasn't an instant fix. Rosa didn't pick up the phone immediately. But she kept the card.

A week later, she wrote back, her own words tentative but honest, *"I miss you too, Eve. I've missed you for a long time. Your words meant a lot."*

That exchange was the first plank in what became *"The Bridge Called Grace."* It took many more conversations, some tearful, some awkward, as they navigated the debris of their past hurt. They had to learn to speak to each other again, listen without interrupting, and offer words of understanding even when the memories were painful.

Evelyn had to own her part truly, and Rosa had to find it in her heart to provide the grace for forgiveness, not because the hurt magically vanished, but because the desire to restore their sisterhood finally outweighed the need to be right. Their words, chosen with newfound care and steeped in a mutual longing for reconciliation, slowly, painstakingly, rebuilt the connection that harsh words had once shattered. They learned that grace, expressed through humble, honest words, could indeed bridge the widest of divides.

Words of grace are also essential for restoration. Grace involves extending kindness, understanding, and a second chance, even when it feels completely undeserved. It's choosing to see the best in someone, even when they've shown you their worst.

It's speaking words of acceptance, not condemnation…

It's saying, *"I see your flaws, I see your mistakes, and I choose to extend kindness and acceptance anyway, because you are more than your worst moment."*

This is powerful among families, in friendships, and especially in a world that's quick to judge and slow to forgive.

From the Ashes: Words That Rebuild

Beyond healing personal hurts and restoring fractured relationships, words possess the power to rebuild entire lives, communities, and dreams that have been shattered. This is where the language of possibility, that powerful force we discussed earlier, becomes the blueprint for reconstruction after devastation.

When someone has taken a major hit—*lost a job, a business fails, or a personal crisis hits hard—their world can feel like it has crumbled.*

Their confidence is often in ruins, and their inner voice might be screaming, "It's over. You're done. You'll never get back on your feet." In those moments, the words from others and those they choose to speak to themselves are vital building materials for starting over.

Words of encouragement:

"You've got this. This isn't the end; it's just a detour. You're stronger than you think. I've seen your resilience."

Words of belief:

"I still believe in you. I've seen what you can do, even when you can't see it yourself."

Words of vision:

"What if this isn't the end, but a chance to build something even better, something more aligned with who you are now?"

Words of practical support, offered with empathy and without judgment:

"How can I help? What do you need right now? Let's take it one step at a time."

Think about my friend, **Jessica**. She had poured everything she had – *her time, her money, her heart and soul – into opening a small bookstore in our town.*

It was her dream, her passion project. But between online competition and a tough economy, it failed within two years. She was heartbroken, financially wiped out, and felt like a complete and utter failure.

Her self-talk was brutal:

"You're an idiot. You wasted everything. You're not cut out for this. You'll never be good at anything."

For weeks, she hardly stepped outside her house. Her friends made lovely efforts to cheer her up, but nothing seemed to work.

Then, one day, her wonderful old college professor, **Dr. Evans**, who had always nurtured her passion for literature, reached out with a call. He had heard about the bookstore closing. He didn't offer business advice or try to tell her what she should have done differently. He simply talked about books, stories, and how every great narrative includes moments of loss, of falling apart, and of the hero hitting rock bottom; yet, that's often where the real story begins—*where the character discovers their true strength.*

"Jessica," he said, his voice calm and steady, full of genuine care.

"A bookstore might have been the stage, but your gift isn't just selling books. Your gift is connecting people to stories, to ideas, to hope, to other worlds. That's still in you. A balance sheet can't take that away."

He didn't instruct her next steps; instead, he reminded her of her true self. He emphasised her gift and passion beyond the failed business. He revitalised her identity as someone who connects people through stories and shares light through literature.

His words, combined with the gentle, nonjudgmental presence of friends who simply showed up to sit with her, watch movies, and be with her in her pain, began to plant seeds of possibility. Jessica didn't open another bookstore; instead, she launched a literary podcast, interviewing authors and discussing the books she loved.

She also started hosting small pop-up book events in local cafes, bringing the personal touch she loved about her store to new spaces. It wasn't the dream she lost but a new dream built on the same foundation of her passion for stories and connection.

Dr. Evans' words, and the new words she started speaking to herself, *"I am a connector, my gift is still valuable–this is a chance to build differently."*

It became the first step in rebuilding her purpose and identity, reminding her that her core gift remained intact, ready to be used anew…

The ability of words to heal is essential in communities experiencing difficulties. Following a natural disaster, the closure of a factory that impacts a town, or a time of social unrest that disrupts community bonds, the language used by leaders, organizers, and ordinary people becomes energetic.

Words of unity, resilience, shared purpose, and hope can galvanize people to work together, support each other, and rebuild not just physical structures but the very fabric of their community: trust and a sense of belonging.

Conversely, *words of blame, despair, or division* can keep wounds open, prevent progress, and leave the community stuck in the wreckage.

The Whisper of the Impossible: Speaking Life When There Seems to Be None

We've talked about healing personal hurts, restoring fractured relationships, and rebuilding after setbacks. These are powerful acts— *acts of faith in action.*

But what about the situations that feel truly impossible?

The ones where hope seems like a cruel joke?

When the odds are so high, they feel impossible, and reason indicates there's no escape?

This is where words spoken in *faith*, even when everything looks bleak, hold a power that can feel almost *miraculous*. It's the parent who receives a devastating diagnosis for their child but chooses to utter words of hope and belief in healing, expressions of faith in a power greater than the illness, even as they pursue every medical option.

It's the person facing insurmountable debt who begins to declare financial freedom and seek creative solutions, articulating abundance out of lack. It's the community fighting against systemic injustice that continues to speak the truth and demand change, proclaiming freedom from oppression, even when the system seems unbreakable.

> *"Faith doesn't ask to be seen. It only asks to be spoken!"*
> **– Proverb**

These words aren't about denying reality. They focus on a different truth—*the truth of possibility, resilience, and a power greater than the current circumstances.*

They declare what can be, spoken out loud, into the teeth of what is. They are the language of faith, said with conviction, believing that what you voice, you attract.

My journey shared in this book has been a constant dance with this…

There have been moments, dark nights of the soul, when the negative voices, both inside and out, felt overwhelming. Times when speaking life, when declaring a different reality, seemed like a ridiculous exercise in self-delusion, as if I was just talking to myself in an empty room.

Yet something—*a flicker of stubborn faith, a memory of my father's words, a deep-down knowing that words do have power—kept me going.*

It led me to choose the words of possibility over despair, the words of faith over fear… because ultimately, "If you don't like what you are reaping, you must change what you are sowing!"

It's not a magic formula that makes everything easy…

It doesn't mean you won't face pain or setbacks. *It doesn't mean you just say the words and poof!* Everything is fixed. However, the consistent act of choosing words that align with healing, restoration, and rebuilding for yourself and others is where the ground begins to shift. That's where the impossible begins to feel like a challenge you can overcome.

As we close this chapter, reflecting on the capacity of words to mend and build a new one, I hear my father's firm voice echoing the wisdom of generations:

"The same tongue that speaks the problem can speak the solution."

The power does not lie outside us in some uncontrollable force; it resides within us. It exists in our speech and the words we select.

We've seen the destructive power of words, how they can control us, and how our own inner words can imprison us. But now, we've seen the other side—their breathtaking capacity for good, for mending the deepest hurts, for bringing back what was lost, for building dreams from dust.

This power truly exists; it's within your reach; it belongs to you!

But understanding it isn't enough…

Reading about it won't change a single thing on its own…

True transformation occurs in action, in choice, and in the everyday—*sometimes even hourly—decisions to wield this remarkable power not for harm, not for criticism, and not for destruction, but for…*

Thank you for all we've discussed!

It's been about healing, restoring, rebuilding, and bringing life to those areas that once felt lifeless…

And that, my friends, is where we're headed next!

We're diving into the practical application, creating a habit out of this incredible power. Imagine living a life where positive, intentional words aren't just a lovely thought, but truly the air we breathe and the ground we walk on.

But before we get there, before we dive into the final, ultimate challenge, there's one last piece of the puzzle. One final, critical element that unlocks the full, explosive potential of words to transform everything.

It's something so simple, so fundamental, yet so often overlooked in our noisy, fast-paced world. It's the quiet force that amplifies every word of healing, every phrase of restoration, every declaration of rebuilding, turning them from mere sounds into unstoppable forces of change.

What is this missing piece?

What is the most powerful ingredient that makes words come alive and reshape reality in profound ways?

It's not just about speaking right words; it's about their origin and the power behind them. Aligning your words with something so fundamental can move mountains, part seas, and bring the dead back to life.

And the truth is that you already have access to it; you might not realize it…

Get ready… Because understanding this…

It's not just a game-changer…

It changes absolutely everything…

This book is, at last, but learning from life never ends…

Chapter 10
Make Positive Words a Daily Habit

"We are what we repeatedly do. Excellence, then, is not an act, but a habit." – **Aristotle**

Standing here at the edge of this final chapter, my heart feels full. It seems like just yesterday I sat down, a little scared and a little unsure, with a blank page staring back at me. The idea was simple, almost too simple: ***Words.***

<u>Could they really matter that much?</u>

<u>Could something as common as the sounds we make and the thoughts we think truly shape a life?</u>

Writing this book has been more than just putting words on paper; it has been a journey through my own life, reflecting on times when words uplifted me and when they hurt me deeply. It has involved listening to the subtle whispers in my mind and discerning between the voice of fear and the voice of truth.

We've journeyed down this path together, discovering the amazing landscape of words. We've noticed how they act like the unseen architects of our reality, always shaping the world around us.

We've felt the vibrant energy they hold, knowing that every single word creates a ripple, influencing not just our lives, but everyone around us too. We bravely spoke the language of faith and possibility, recognising that voicing our dreams is the crucial first step towards making them a reality.

We faced the hard truth that words can wound, leaving scars that linger long after the sound fades. We talked about the slow, brave work of healing from those hurts. We wrestled with the challenge of controlling our own tongues, learning that sometimes silence is the strongest word, and that peace often begins with a single, mindful pause.

We celebrated the power of words in the lives of those who have achieved greatness, seeing how they spoke their victories into existence. And we turned inward, shining a light on the most important conversation of all: the one we have with ourselves, recognizing that our inner dialogue is the foundation of our self-worth.

You've learned that words are not just sounds or symbols but living forces. They are the seeds you plant in the garden of your life, and whatever you grow, you will eventually harvest. You've seen that the most important conversation you have is in your head and that controlling your tongue is key to finding peace, both within yourself and with others.

But knowing all this, understanding it in your head and feeling it in your heart, is just the beginning of the journey. It's like knowing how to build a beautiful house by reading every book on architecture and construction. You understand the principles, you know the tools, and you can draw the blueprints—but the house doesn't appear, doesn't become a home, until you start putting in the work, day after day, brick by brick, nail by nail.

This final chapter isn't about introducing new concepts or theories; it's about taking everything we've learned and making it real, making it a part of who you are. It's about moving from *understanding* the power of words to *living* the power of words. It's about making the conscious, deliberate, and consistent choice to speak life, choose wisely, and build with intention, not just sometimes, when it's easy, but every single day, especially when it's hard.

This is where the real, lasting transformation begins – *in the simple, consistent habits you create the small choices you make repeatedly.*

A Daily Commitment: Speaking Life

With startling clarity, we've seen how powerful words are, for both incredibly good and devastating harm.

Now comes the final, most important call in this book:

A profound commitment to use that power for the highest good, starting today, in this very moment, and continuing tomorrow, and the day after that, for the rest of your life.

It's a commitment to speaking life into the quiet corners of your heart, the sacred spaces of your relationships, the challenges of your work, and the vast, interconnected world around you.

Speaking life daily means choosing words that are not empty sounds, but intentional forces. It means choosing words that:

- ***Build:*** Words that lift up, encourage, and strengthen the spirit, both yours and others. Think of them as a home's sturdy beams and walls, providing structure and support.

- ***Heal:*** Words that soothe, comfort, and mend the broken or wounded places. These gentle hands tend to emotional cuts and bruises, allowing them to close and scar over, becoming stronger.

- ***Empower:*** Words that instil confidence, courage, and unwavering belief in potential. These sparks ignite courage, reminding you and others of the strength that lies within, ready to face any challenge.

- ***Connect:*** Words that foster understanding, empathy, and love, bridging gaps and building bridges between hearts and minds. They are the threads that weave the tapestry of human connection, making us feel seen and less alone.

- ***Create:*** Words that declare possibility, vision, and purpose, bringing the unseen into the realm of the possible. These are the blueprints of your future, spoken into existence, guiding your steps towards the life you dream of.

It's easy, relatively speaking, to speak life when everything is going well when the sun is shining, and the path is smooth. The real challenge, the place where true power is forged, comes in speaking life when things are hard. When you're bone-tired, when you're overwhelmed with frustration when you've stumbled and made a mistake you regret, when someone has spoken words that have hurt you deeply.

That's when choosing words of patience, forgiveness, resilience, and unwavering hope becomes an act of profound strength and courage. That's when your words become a lifeline, pulling you and others towards the shore.

This daily commitment isn't about pretending everything is perfect or putting on a fake smile to mask real pain. It's about choosing your focus, even in the midst of difficulty. It's about acknowledging the challenges, hurt, and setbacks while still consciously declaring your inner strength and capacity to overcome.

It's about recognizing the pain while actively speaking healing into that space. It's about seeing the world as it is, with all its flaws and difficulties, while actively speaking the globe you want to create into existence, holding that vision steady with your words.

It's a conscious, deliberate, moment-by-moment decision. Before a word leaves your lips, before a thought takes root in your mind, ***you ask...***

Will this word build?

Will this thought empower?

Will this sentence bring peace?

This is the practice...

This is the commitment that changes everything...

The Ripple Effect of Small Changes: Creating a Wave of Goodness

You might still have that little voice, maybe from somewhere deep inside, whispering, *"Okay, but how much difference can my few words, my small choices, really make in the grand scheme of things? The world is so big, so loud, so full of negativity."* And I understand that feeling. I've felt it, too. But the answer, I promise you, is an enormous, ***immeasurable difference.***

Reflect on the concept of words carrying energy and creating ripples. It's not just a gentle disturbance; it's a force that spreads. A single stone, even a small one, dropped into a vast, still pond sends waves across the entire surface, reaching shores far from where the stone first broke the water. Your words work the exact same way. They are not ***isolated events***; they are ***catalysts***.

While choosing a calm, measured tone and a few thoughtful words instead of snapping in frustration can completely change the atmosphere of your home or workplace in that moment. It prevents a small moment of tension from escalating into a major conflict, saving emotional energy and preserving peace— *A seemingly small change in how you respond to stress.*

A small, consistent change in your self-talk – replacing that automatic, harsh *"I always mess up"* with a more truthful and empowering *"I'm learning and improving with every step"* – can fundamentally shift your mindset from defeat and limitation to growth and possibility. This subtle internal shift, repeated over and over, changes how you approach challenges, how resilient you are in the face of setbacks, and ultimately, what you believe you can achieve.

It's the difference between staying stuck and moving forward...

A small word of genuine appreciation or a simple, heartfelt thank you offered to a colleague, a friend, or a family member can brighten their entire day, boost their morale in a quiet but powerful way, and strengthen the bonds of your relationship. That positive energy, that feeling of being seen and valued, doesn't just stop with them; it can then spread to others they interact with, creating a chain reaction of kindness.

These aren't dramatic, headline-grabbing events that make the news. They are the quiet, consistent, almost invisible acts of choosing positive words that build a life, day by day, interaction by interaction, thought by thought.

The cumulative effect of these small, intentional changes is profound. They reshape your internal landscape, clearing away the weeds of doubt and fear. They reshape your relationships, building stronger, more resilient connections. And they contribute, in a very real way, to the collective energy of the world around you, adding light instead of shadow.

This is the incredible, often underestimated power of habit...

A single positive word might seem small, almost insignificant at the moment, but a thousand positive words, spoken consistently over time, can literally reshape your reality from the inside out. Just as negative words, repeated, can wear you down, erode your confidence, and limit your potential, positive words, repeated, can build you up into someone stronger, more confident, more resilient, and more at peace than you ever thought possible.

It's not magic; it's the power of consistent, intentional action…

Building a Lifelong Habit: Practical Steps for a Powerful Life

So, how do you turn this deep understanding and heartfelt commitment into a deeply ingrained, almost automatic habit?

How do you make speaking life as natural and effortless as breathing?

It takes practice, patience, and simple, repeatable actions that you weave into the fabric of your daily life. It's not about adding complicated tasks to your already busy schedule; it's about shifting how you think and speak.

Here are some practical steps, drawn from the wisdom we've explored, to help you make speaking life a natural and powerful part of your everyday existence:

1. Start Your Day with Intention (and a Declaration): The first few moments of your day set the tone for everything that follows. Before you even reach for your phone, the worries of the day rush in, and you get caught up in the to-do list. Take a moment to speak a few intentional words about the day ahead. This isn't about forcing yourself to feel happy if you don't; it's about setting a tone, declaring your approach, and directing your energy.

- *Try saying aloud or in your mind:* "Today, I choose peace, no matter what comes." "I am capable of handling whatever challenges cross my path today." "I will look for opportunities to speak kindness and encouragement to others." "I am grateful for this new day and its possibilities." This simple practice, taking just a minute or two, directs your mind and spirit

116

towards possibility and resilience.

2. *Become a Self-Talk Detective (with Compassion):* Throughout the day, notice the conversations happening in your head. What are you telling yourself about your abilities, worth, challenges, appearance, past, and future? Notice the patterns without judgment at first. Think of yourself as a gentle observer of your own thoughts, not a harsh critic.

- Keep a small notebook, use a notes app on your phone, or even make a mental note to jot down recurring negative phrases or beliefs. Just seeing them written down, or even acknowledging them, can give your perspective and lessen their power over you. You might be surprised how often certain phrases repeat.

3. *Reframe Negative Thoughts Immediately (and with Truth):* Once you catch a negative thought, don't just let it sit there and fester. Consciously challenge its validity and replace it with a more truthful, balanced, or empowering statement. This is where you actively rewrite your internal script.

- ***If you catch yourself thinking:*** "I'm so overwhelmed, there's no way I can get all this done." *Pause, take a breath, and reframe it as:* "This is a lot, but I will take it one step at a time. I can handle this moment, and I will focus on the next right thing."

- ***If you think:*** "I messed up again. I'm so stupid." *Pause, and reframe it as:* "Okay, that didn't go as planned. Mistakes are how I learn and grow. What can I learn from this experience?"

- ***If you think:*** "I'm not good enough." *Reframe it as:* "I am enough, just as I am, and I am always learning and growing." This isn't about denying reality, but about choosing a perspective that empowers you rather than defeats you.

4. Use Affirmations Consistently (with Feeling): Choose a few affirmations that truly resonate with you – statements about who you are, who you are becoming, or the qualities you want to embody. Repeat them throughout the day, especially when you face challenges, moments of doubt, or feel your energy dipping.

- **Examples:** "I am strong and resilient." "I am worthy of love and happiness." "I am capable of achieving my goals." "I attract abundance and positive opportunities." "I am at peace with myself and the world." Speak them aloud if you can, feeling the vibration of the words. If you can't speak aloud, repeat them silently in your mind, focusing on the feeling behind the words. The key is repetition, consistency, and connecting with the truth you are declaring.

5. Practice the Pause (Again and Again and Again): This is so important it bears repeating. Take a breath before you respond in a conversation, especially when emotions are high, when you feel defensive, angry, or frustrated. That tiny pause, just a second or two, gives you the crucial space to choose your words instead of reacting impulsively from a place of emotion.

- **Make it a physical reminder:** Put a sticky note on your computer, your phone, your steering wheel, or anywhere you'll see it often that just says "PAUSE." In conversations, visualize a stop sign before you speak. This simple habit can prevent unnecessary hurt and regret.

6. Speak Kindness to Others Daily (Intentionally): Make a conscious effort to offer a genuine compliment, a word of sincere encouragement, a simple thank you, or a word of validation to at least one person each day. This isn't about flattery; it's about seeing the good in others and acknowledging it. This practice not only brightens their day and strengthens their relationships but also reinforces their own habit of speaking life and looking for the positive.

- *It could be as simple as:* "I really appreciate your help with that; it made a big difference." "You handled that situation really well." "That's a great idea; I hadn't thought of that." "Thank you for listening."

7. End Your Day with Gratitude and Reflection (Focusing on the Good): Before you drift off to sleep, take a few moments to reflect on your day. Instead of dwelling on what went wrong, what you didn't accomplish, or what someone said that bothered you, consciously focus on what went right, what you learned, what you are grateful for, and how you used your words for good. Acknowledge your efforts, even the small ones.

- *Ask yourself:* "What is one positive word I used today, either to myself or someone else?" "What is one kind thing I said or thought today?" "What am I thankful for in this moment?" "What is one small step I took today that I'm proud of?" This practice rewires your brain to end the day positively, reinforcing the habit of looking for the good.

8. Be Patient and Compassionate with Yourself (Always): Let me repeat this, and please hear it deeply: You will not do this perfectly. There will be days when you slip up when you say something you regret, when that negative inner voice screams louder than you'd like. That is okay. That is part of being human. Don't use those moments as an excuse for more negative self-talk. Don't let a stumble turn into a fall. Simply notice what happened without harsh judgment, learn from the experience, and gently, compassionately recommit to the practice. Treat yourself with the same understanding, kindness, and patience you would offer a dear friend who is learning something new and challenging. Your journey is one of progress, not perfection.

Making positive words a daily habit is like training a muscle that has been weak or unused for a long time. It feels awkward and difficult at first, maybe even a little painful. But with consistent exercise, with daily practice, it becomes stronger, more natural, and eventually, it becomes a source of incredible power and ease. The more you practice, the easier it becomes, and the more you'll see the undeniable, beautiful results unfolding in your life.

Your Challenge: What Words Will You Choose?

And so, we arrive at the end of these pages, but not the end of the story. This is the final call. The knowledge is here, the tools have been shared, and the path is laid out before you, stretching into the future. The only thing left, the most important element, is the choice. Your choice.

The power of words is not a secret held by a select few; it is a force woven into the very fabric of existence, available to everyone, including you. But it is a force that requires conscious direction, intention, and will.

Without your mindful awareness and deliberate choice, your words can drift, influenced by fear, old habits, the negativity of the world around you, or the echoes of the past. But with your intention, with your conscious choice, your words become powerful instruments of creation, healing, connection, and peace.

So, as you close this book, as you take a deep breath and look ahead, I leave you with this personal, profound challenge, the heart of everything we've explored:

What words will you choose today?

You wake in the stillness of morning, and before the world makes its demands, a quiet voice stirs within. *What will I say to myself today?* In the moments no one sees, when the weight feels heavy and the path unclear, you hear it again—*Speak strength... Speak life...The choice is yours...*

When tension rises, and everything inside you screams to give up, your soul leans in and whispers, You were made for more. You stand in front of the mirror, eyes locking with your own, and you don't flinch. You say what you once feared: I am enough. I am worthy. I am capable.

When tempers flare, and silence could cut out in the world, you steady yourself and respond—not with more noise, but with grace. Not with bitterness but with power. The kind of power that heals. The type of power that builds bridges and mends hearts. Because you know what you carry, you know your words are not just sounds—they are *seeds, weapons, and light.*

You build up instead of tearing down. You choose to speak with faith rather than echoing fear. You opt for gratitude instead of spiraling into complaint. Rather than pointing fingers, you extend compassion. You rise up in possibility instead of drowning in doubt.

Now that you understand, remember this too: *Whatever You Voice, You Attract!*

Your words are actively shaping your life—moment by moment, day by day. They not only sculpt your destiny but also mold your relationships, empower your strength, and resonate into your legacy.

This is your turning point...

Right here...

Right now...

You carry a truth that can move mountains and rewrite stories.

Speak Power...

Speak Truth...

Speak boldly...

Speak with love...

Your future is listening...

So, speak...

And...

Watch the impossible unfold...

No Retreat...

No Surrender...

It's an and, but not an end...

www.ingramcontent.com/pod-product-compliance
Lightning Source LLC
Chambersburg PA
CBHW051213120626
46547CB00013B/1332